information utilities

prentice-hall series in automatic computation
george forsythe, editor

A nurse using a CRT terminal which is part of a hospital information utility (see page 33). Courtesy Sanders Associates

information utilities

richard e. sprague, president,
personal data services corporation

prentice-hall, incorporated,
englewood cliffs, new jersey

© 1969 by prentice-hall, inc.,
englewood cliffs, new jersey

all rights reserved—no part of this book
may be reproduced in any form
or by any means without permission
in writing from the publisher

1 2 3 4 5 6 7 8 9 10   current printing (first digit)

13-464693-2

library of congress catalog card number 72-95707

london: prentice-hall international, inc.
sydney: prentice-hall of australia, pty. ltd.
toronto: prentice-hall of canada, ltd.
new delhi: prentice-hall of india private ltd.
tokyo: prentice-hall of japan, inc.

printed in the united states of america

acknowledgments

This book took its inspiration from several sources. Its roots are to be found in my book *Electronic Business Systems— Management Use of On-Line Real-Time Computers* (New York: The Ronald Press, 1962), especially in Chapters 2 and 3, which described the pressures forcing development of shared on line–real time systems. Others saw the same pressures: as early as 1963 Jaap Unk (of ISYS, Philips, the University of Delft, and the University of Utah) was convinced that information utilities would soon be a subject of major importance. Martin Greenberger, then with MIT's Project MAC and now at the Johns Hopkins University, influenced many of the basic ideas, as well as the selection of the title. The success of Keydata Corporation and the enthusiasm of Charlie Adams, Bill Emmons, and Joe Weinrebe were significant ingredients.

The research work and support of Roger Crane and the entire Advanced Business Systems staff at Touche, Ross, Bailey & Smart were invaluable. Special thanks for assistance go to Dennis Lytle and the late Sherman Blumenthal. Chapter 4 (on SAVE) is derived from several sources at TRB & S, primarily from the work of Sherman Blumenthal, Bob Head, and Bob Stevens. Credit must go to Jack Quinn for the creative energy which makes it possible to describe an operating ticketing system in Chapter 5.

contents

prediction

Before the twentieth century ends, an information revolution will be in full swing.[1] *It will not be the highly publicized, over-dramatized computer revolution of the 1960's. Rather, it will be a revolution in the way human beings think, learn, reason, and act.*

It will be made possible by a marriage of minds and machines. The impact on you, the reader, as an individual will be direct—not indirect, as has been the impact of computers on most of us.

---

1. "The Information Revolution" was described in an article of that name in *The New York Times'* Sunday Supplement, May 23, 1965, in connection with IFIP Congress 65.

You will, through the use of information utility services in your home, your office, your library, your classroom, and in many public service locations, begin to think and act differently. The impact on you will be far greater than the combined effect of television and the telephone.

The chief difference in this revolution is that information will be interactively related to your own personal life and to the way your mind works, especially your memory. The television set imparts information, but you do not interact with it directly. The information utilities of the future, and even some today, will interact with your memory and other mental processes as well as with many of your physical activities which deal primarily with information. The interaction will be immediate in whatever location you find yourself. You will communicate with the utility and it will communicate with you. Together, the combination will produce some startling and revolutionary results.

Your everyday problems will diminish. Many types of transactions now very lengthy and confused will become simpler. Your memory will improve. If you so desire, your logical and reasoning ability will improve. Your learning capacity and speed will increase. You will, if you are so inclined, be able to better understand your own mental processes, through a kind of self-organizing analysis of the way you think, reason, remember, plan, and make decisions.

For some, this revolution may seem to be dangerous, a kind of 1984 in high gear. The old bugaboo of machines or robots taking over will be raised. Nevertheless, the revolution will take place, as all others have, because it is "a natural." Humans who take advantage of the revolution, who help bring it about, will just naturally win out over those who do not.

This book describes the genesis of the revolution, already in the sixth or seventh year of development: the information utility.

part i   concept and market

Part i introduces the concept of an information utility by using the analogy of the telephone system and by giving a detailed technical definition. An overview of types of utilities is presented from the point of view of marketing information utility services.

This part of the book will be of special interest to current or potential owners and operators of utilities. A rather startling impression is presented of the very large number of existing utility services. For those skeptical of the IU concept— those who maintain it is off in the far distant future—these overview and marketing chapters should be quite novel.

1 concept, history, and definitions

history

The first use of the term *information utilities* appears to have been made by Professor Martin Greenberger in the July 1964 article titled "The Computers of Tomorrow."[1] He said, "Barring unforeseen obstacles, an on-line interactive computer service, provided commercially by an information utility, may be as commonplace by 2000 A.D. as telephone service is today."

Professor Jaap Unk referred to information utilities in his article on "Information Centers and Computer Utilities" in August 1964.[2] The author's first use of the term was in the article "Information Utilities," published in April 1965[3] and October 1965.[4] The impact of the concept was described in the article "Electronic Business Systems—1984."[5]

In the succeeding years an ever-increasing number of articles and books have been published using the terms *information utilities* or *computer utilities*.[6] Two books were published on the subject of computer utilities in 1966–67.[7]

---

1. Martin Greenberger, "The Computers of Tomorrow," *Atlantic Monthly*, July, 1964.

2. J. M. Unk, "Information Centers and Computer Utilities," in *Information Centers as a Public Utility* (The Hague: ISYS, 1964).

3. Richard E. Sprague, "Information Utilities," *Business Automation*, April, 1965.

4. Richard E. Sprague, "Information Utilities," *Financial Executive*, October, 1965.

5. Richard E. Sprague, "Electronic Business Systems — 1984," *Business Automation*, February, 1966.

6. The October 1968 issue of *Computing Reviews*, the Association for Computing Machinery publication, contains a comprehensive bibliography on the subject of computer utilities, compiled by Michael A. Duggan.

7. B. R. Anderson, *et al., Future of the Computer Utility* (New York: American Management Association, 1967); and D. F. Parkhill, *Challenge of the Computer Utility* (Reading, Mass.: Addison-Wesley Publishing Co., 1966).

The historical developments leading to information utilities might be thought of in phases:

Phase 1: The appearance of the electronic computer

Phase 2: The coupling of data communications, terminals, and computers to build on line–real time systems

Phase 3: The sharing of on line–real time systems among many user organizations

Phase 4: The development of time sharing

Phase 5: The commercialization of information utility services

Phase 6: The true human–utility interactive phase

Some of these phases overlap, and the numbers do not in every case indicate the true chronology. Certain information utility services, such as computer aided instruction (CAI) and engineering problem solving time sharing, have already entered Phase 6. Others, such as airline reservations, are just entering Phase 3 and may never develop beyond that.

The importance and recognition of the information utility concept can best be measured by the hearings being held by the FCC on the subject of communications and data processing. The hearings were initiated in 1966 and will probably continue for a few more years. The regulatory groups expressing an interest include the Antitrust Division of the Justice Department, the various government agencies given regulatory powers by the Brooks Bill, and many financially oriented agencies.

The major problem areas lie in the domain of the information utility. At stake are the regulatory policies which may govern or affect all communications, computer, and information utility organizations. The FCC itself may be altered, or may become subservient to a super-governmental agency aimed at IU regulation of all types.

the information utility concept

Information utilities may be thought of as one class of on line–real time systems in which a large number of individual users from many different organizations will be sharing a central data processing and memory complex. Each user will be supplied with a data terminal, or input-output device, connected directly to the center at the time of use. Time sharing computing centers are examples of information utilities. A more precise definition of an information utility is given later in this chapter.

fundamental change in computer use

The information utility and time sharing developments, while in their infancy, are moving so fast and in so many different directions at once, it is difficult to see what may happen. However, following the "where there is smoke, there is fire" theory, it seems certain that we can base some predictions on the reality of the concepts for the future. Current trends, in fact, lead us to believe (as we said in the Prediction) that a fundamental change in the utilization of computers and information has already begun.

Several other writers have previously made predictions on this change. Here are some quotations from the aforementioned publication of IFIP Congress 65 in May 1965.[8] This *New York Times* supplement was prepared for the public by IFIP Congress 65 to tell the true story of "The Information Revolution" as nearly as possible in layman's terms.

Isaac Auerbach, then President of IFIP, said in his opening article on "Information—A Prime Resource":

"I predicted (in 1962) that the computer and its application to information processing 'will have a far greater constructive impact on mankind during the remainder of the Twentieth Century than any other technological development of the past two decades.' The impact will be felt for many centuries."

Edwin Harder, then Chairman of the Board of Governors, American Federation of Information Processing Societies

8. "The Information Revolution," *The New York Times* Sunday Supplement, May 23, 1965. Edited and published by IFIP Congress 65 in connection with the Congress held at the New York Hilton Hotel, May 24–29, 1965. Reprints available from AFIPS, 211 East 43rd Street, New York, N.Y. 10017.

(the US member of IFIP), stated in his article, "The Myth of the Giant Brain":

"What are the implications (of computers) for adults who in many ways are falling behind their children in understanding the changes taking place in our world today? Simply this: the computer *is* an understandable tool—and it has become so important a tool, with so much potential for changing our lives and our world, that it may be more important for the average man to understand how a computer works than how his automobile works. . . . Within the next decade, these machines will affect our lives more than any other technological development in history. They have given mankind new and efficient ways of looking at and solving problems. They have created new professions and new philosophies of management and have made possible whole new industries. They affect us all, because of their influence on economic planning and our manual solution, their ability as *general purpose* tools to better our lives in literally countless ways."

Ulric Neisser, associate professor at Brandeis University, wrote on "Information and Men":

"The new techniques of processing information will cease to be the property of a few specialists and become accessible to all. With the present accelerated pace of technical and social change, the development of "time shared" computers with remote terminals will proceed rapidly. In the not-too-distant future, ordinary people of every sort will use these devices in their daily affairs: at the office, at the library, at school and eventually in their homes."

And, finally, Simon Ramo, of TRW, Inc., and Bunker-Ramo Corporation, says in his article on "The Computer as an Intellectual Tool":

"The mass extension of man's intellect by machine and the partnership of man and machine in the handling of information may well be the technological advance dominating this century. As the total information handling capacity of the world grows through the new partnership, the total brain-power of man is expanded. Industry, government, and all of the professions will be greatly altered, and so thus, will be society. . . . The next decade or two will see an even broader penetration of the computer and associated electronic systems into every facet of society's endeavors in which informational and intellectual activity exists."

The dominant theme in these quotations is highlighted by Ramo's word, partnership. Until now, most readers have probably not thought about forming a partnership with a computer, or even communicating in any way with a computer. It has been like some mysterious instrument used by highly trained specialists, affecting you as an individual only indirectly through your company or by a computer generated bill received from your department store or telephone company.

Well, that is all going to change, and in some places, like schools, change very rapidly. By the end of the century we will all be communicating directly with computer systems. The form of communication will be quite different from what it has been for programmers or computer operators until recently. We will be "talking to" the computers in our own language, and they will be responding in our language, literally by voice in some cases.

We will be connected, on line, to the computers through simple devices located in places where we usually go. The telephone in our home or on our office desk could be such a device. We will be exchanging information, putting information away for safe keeping, retrieving it again, solving problems, extending our memories, receiving informational and financial services, and, in general, acting in concert or partnership with computer systems.

The commercial services and information centers that will make all of this possible are information utilities. The stimulus for their development will, as usual, be primarily economic factors and private enterprise profit making.

The owners may range widely from the federal government to small businessmen. Various sociological, legal, and business regulatory changes will have to take place during this new revolution. Successive chapters in the book discuss the possible types, owners, impact, sociological problems, and technological status of information utilities.

other names

Several other names have been used to describe the information utility concept. Time-shared systems have already been mentioned. On-line shared systems, on-line service bureaus, data banks, and information retrieval centers are terms also used. The relationships and differences among all of these terms require clarification.

The word "utility" in the term *information utility* is derived from the public utility in which the commodity or service is provided to many subscribers in the quantity and at the time and place needed. Electrical power, gas, water, and telephone service fall into this category. The fact that utilities are regulated by government agencies is incidental to this definition and concept. There is no reason to assume that all information utilities will be regulated. In fact, those now in existence are *not* regulated.

The word "information" in the title may be too limited, since it implies that the utility is supplying information only. In actuality, the utility may be supplying computational, problem solving, financial, and other services. In connection with information services, the collection, sorting, processing, storage, analyzing, and display of information may be involved. The definition in this book is that the information utility "supplies a service to many subscribers which is, in one way or another, related to information." From this point on, the word "information" will encompass all of these services.

The key words in the public utility derivation mentioned earlier are: "in the *quantity* and at the *time* and *place* needed." The quantity of information a subscriber may need at any given time could be as small as a single, simple, one word answer or as large as a complete text. He may purchase just the amount he needs and no more.

The subscriber will receive the information at the time he demands it or at scheduled times when he needs it. Furthermore, the delay between the time a subscriber asks for information and the time he receives it will be as short as necessary to meet his requirements. Thus, a response time may be as short as a fraction of a second or a few seconds in many cases.

Finally, the place where the subscriber needs the information may be his home, his office, or other normal places of business. These last two features (time and place) are the parts of the definition of an information utility that produce the requirement of an on line–real time system. By analogy, it can be concluded that all four public utility services, electricity, gas, water, and telephone, are on line–real time in nature.

Herein lies the difference between an information utility and a normal data processing service bureau. The utility supplies the information directly at the subscriber's own location, in a format that he normally uses in his business or personal life.

Another part of the definition is the method of payment by the subscriber for the services received. As in a public utility, subscribers may pay on a per transaction basis plus an installation charge for the terminals on his premises. If the subscriber stores away information on his own, he will pay a monthly charge proportional to the storage space used.

telephone service analogy

One way of describing or defining an information utility is to compare it to the largest existing utility service in the world, our own telephone service. Table 1-1 lists the characteristics of the US telephone system. It provides both voice and data communications services on a national scale. The service charge structure is based on an installation charge, a monthly base charge per terminal (telephone) and a unit charge for

Table 1-1   Characteristics of telephone system

---

1. Voice and data communications utility
2. Service charge structure—base plus unit transaction
3. Service prompt, reliable, coverage everywhere, available to all
4. Service relatively inexpensive
5. Telephone instrument not purchased or rented by subscriber
6. Computers used, but without subscriber's knowledge
7. Service simple, easily understood, in subscriber's own language
8. Service provided at subscriber's own location

11

each transaction (telephone call), depending on the type. The service is prompt, with response times in fractions of a second. It is supplied everywhere at any desirable subscriber location, whether home, office, or car, and it is available to all. It is relatively inexpensive, and the subscriber purchases as little or as much as he desires. The terminal (the telephone) and all of the equipment involved remain the property of the telephone company and are neither purchased nor rented by the subscriber. If computers or other complex devices are used in providing the telephone service, the subscribers know nothing about it, nor does it matter to them. The service is simple in concept, easily understood and used by laymen, and provided in the subscriber's own language and format. (We exclude here the problem of the housewife who does not understand direct distance dialing.)

information utility characteristics

If we transfer these characteristics by analogy into those of an information utility listed in Table 1-2, it can be seen that

Table 1-2   Information utility characteristics

---

1. Central on line–real time facility
2. Many subscribers at remote locations
3. Information storage, retrieval, processing, and computing provided
4. Services provided at subscriber's own location
5. Service simple to understand and use and in subscriber's own language
6. Service fast, immediate, and reliable — two-way communication
7. Service relatively inexpensive
8. Charges for service on a base plus unit transaction
9. Terminal devices tailored to subscriber's own requirements
10. Knowledge of computers, systems, or programming not needed by subscriber
11. Question and answer mode available — subscriber-system partnership
12. Availability in some utilities for subscriber to set up files, write and check programs
13. Utility responsible for equipment, reliability, file protection, and control

---

most of those on the telephone list carry over to the information utility list.

An IU will have at its heart a centrally located facility with on line–real time capabilities, direct access files, central data communications equipment, and multiprocessing computers.

Like the telephone system, there will be many subscribers at locations remote from the center. Each subscriber has access to a terminal connected directly to the center. The services provided, including storage, retrieval, processing, and computing, will be available at the subscriber's own natural location through his terminal.

The language used by the subscriber will be his own. In fact, it will not make sense to talk about a language except for those services which include programming and program testing at the subscriber's terminal. Just as the housewife does not think about languages when she dials a connection, so the average subscriber to an information utility will not think about languages. The service will be simple to understand and use and will be provided in the subscriber's natural format and environment.

As in the case of telephone service, the IU service will provide fast response, reliability, and two-way communication between subscriber and center. This bidirectional facility will be important in several ways. First, it will permit a dialogue to take place in which the center can direct or control the subscriber's actions as well as answer his questions. This element is very important   controlling the accuracy of the information generated by the subscriber, as well as in leading him through an unstructured sequence of steps. Second, it will allow the subscriber to ask a series of questions or enter bits of information, where each step is analyzed by the center and successive steps or questions are dependent on the preceding ones.

The IU service will be inexpensive. This term, of course, is relative. Each transaction will be low priced, because many subscribers are sharing the cost of the center. A well-known principle of today's computer technology is that the larger and faster the central computing and storage facility, the lower the unit cost of a processed transaction. Information utilities will generally make use of very fast computers and very large mass storage.

A second point with respect to cost is that programming, systems design, installation costs, and many other "hidden" costs associated with a subscriber's own computer installation, are eliminated, from the subscriber's point of view. Of course, such costs are present at the IU center, but they are shared by a large number of subscribers and are built into the service charges. The costs for data communications may also be shared among subscribers to some extent. However, in a metropolitan area served by an IU, those costs for any one subscriber will not be significant.

The subscribers will pay for the IU services on the same basis as the telephone service. They will pay an installation charge for each terminal, probably a base monthly charge whether the service is used or not, a unit charge for each transaction, and a monthly charge for each unit of storage space set aside for the individual subscriber at the center.

In many IU services, the subscriber's terminals will be specially designed to fit the particular group of subscribers. In some cases, such as computer program testing or problem solving, the terminal may be an ordinary teletype machine. In other cases, an ordinary touch tone telephone may be used. In both of these cases, the terminal itself will be quite general purpose in nature and not specially designed. However, the service itself in these cases requires either very limited types of transactions (the touch tone phone) or extensive knowledge about the service (problem solving utility).

Again, except for the problem solving or computer program testing type of service, the subscriber need know nothing about programming or computer systems design. Even the fact that computers are involved at the IU center may not be known.

In the case of *programming* types of services, the subscriber will write and test out his own programs at his terminal, set up his own program and data files at the center, and act as though he has his own computer right in the same room.

There can be an intermediate type of subscriber who sets up files and solves problems but who uses programs already in existence in the center. This subscriber will understand what the programs do but will deal with the IU service in a problem oriented language. He will not generally be writing or testing original programs.

In all cases, the IU has the full responsibility for the equipment and software used to provide the service. It is responsible for reliability, file protection, adequate controls, and audit trails, and any other areas necessary to provide a fast, accurate, reliable service not subject to defalcations.

One question, the answer to which has not been agreed upon by all experts in the field, is whether an on line–real time system in a single organization constitutes an information utility. If many parts of the organization and several different levels of responsibility are users of the system, then it could meet most of the characteristics described so far. A total on line–real time system like the ones being implemented within the larger airlines would be an example.

This book will not include such systems within the definition of an information utility. However, systems shared by several organizations in the same industry, such as ATARS (which is shared by all the airlines), *will* be considered to fall within the definition, as long as the service provided is available to any subscriber in that industry.

All these characteristics, summarized in Table 1-2, constitute the complete definition of an information utility. The next chapter presents an overview of the entire IU situation from the point of view of marketing IU services. Types of utilities and current examples of each type are included.

relationship of IU to other names

From what has been said so far it can be seen how the definition of the words "information utilities" is related to the other names mentioned at the beginning of the chapter. An IU is considered by the author to be one of the class of systems called *on line–real time systems.* Any OLRT system available to be shared by all organizations in the same business or by any broader collection is herein defined as an IU. Any OLRT system used by only one organization or by a limited group of organizations sharing in its ownership generally does not fall within the definition.

Time-shared systems for many individual subscribers are considered by some to be nearly synonymous with IU's. Common usage in the information sciences field tends to confuse the time sharing idea with the IU concept. However, as can be seen from the definition, not all IU's are time sharing systems in the usually accepted sense.

On line–real time *service bureaus* are IU's if they meet the qualification of shared use that has been set by this author. Information retrieval centers operating in an on line–real time mode at remote subscriber points would be a special type of IU.

The term *data bank* has been used by some organizations, notably IBM, to describe the information and the method of storing it in an information utility. However, a "bank" of data stored in one place and made available to many subscribers does not necessarily have to be provided to them in an on-line fashion. If not, a data bank would not be an information utility within this book's definition.

classification by nature and use of files

One other method of classifying OLRT, or time sharing systems, for definitional and clarification purposes seems useful. It was developed and presented by Charles Adams at the Spring Joint Computer Conference in 1966 in Boston.[9] The classification method is shown in Figure 1-1, reprinted from an Adams Associates' pamphlet, distributed at the SJCC. Basically, the idea is to classify the central file information usage.

9. Charles Adams, "The Meanings of Time-Sharing," a pamphlet distributed at the Panel Discussion on The Meanings of Time-Sharing, Spring Joint Computer Conference, Boston, Mass., April 27, 1966.

1. The Data Warehouse offers storage on demand for a single user. While often coupled with an exchange capability to permit sharing procedures or data by selected groups of users, the intent is that the user regard his terminal as his private computer.

   a) `How many potential users of in-house computers will this form of time-sharing garner in the next five to ten years among:

      small users?   none__ some__ many__ most__ all__

      medium users?   none__ some__ many__ most__ all__

      large users?   none__ some__ many__ most__ all__

WAREHOUSE b) Who now offers these services oriented:

      computationally?   IBM, GE, BB&N, Allen-Babcock, Applied Logic, and
      _____

      toward business?   KEYDATA, and _____

2. The Data Supply House, which has been called a Data Bank, provides a source of data for reference by users. It is updated only by the supplier, not by the users.

   a) Data supply house services now in use or imminent include stock market quotations, legal precedent research services, corporate financial histories and economic trends for portfolio analysis, and _____
   _____
   _____

SUPPLY HOUSE b) Promising, but still years from realization, are full-scale library reference services, medical diagnostic aids (or is this a cooperative?), and
   _____
   _____

3. The Data Exchange permits privacy-protected unilateral or bilateral cross-access within what is basically a data warehouse.

   a) Imminent are such applications as hospital in-patient record keeping, commercial factoring, and _____
   _____

   b) Farther away are transfer of credit (the "checkless society"), and
EXCHANGE _____

4. The Data Cooperative represents a pool of information that is both interrogated and updated by the same group of users.

   a) Airline reservations currently fall into this category, along with
   _____
   _____

   b) Less imminent are _____
COOPERATIVE _____

Figure 1-1 Time sharing diagram.
(Reproduced by permission of Adams
Associates, Boston, Massachusetts)

2 *the market*

developmental factors and types

In the late 1960's, two major factors began to combine to create a rapidly growing market for information utility services. The awakening interest on the part of small businesses and individual professionals in automating their accounting and data handling functions was the first factor. Competitive pressures placed on the small businesses by larger firms, which can afford their own information systems, generated much of this interest.

The second factor was the development of the on-line approach to supplying data handling services to a number of small subscribers. Some organizations referred to this approach as *time sharing*. Whatever its name, the approach opened up new possibilities for the subscriber to the service as well as new markets for the supplier.

As an indication of the extent of this market, Table 2-1 is a partial list of the services that emerged. The services are classified according to whether they are general purpose or subscriber oriented, information retrieval applications as opposed to processing applications, digital or graphical. They are also categorized by size of user (small, medium, large) and geographical dispersion (local, regional, national). Table 2-2 (see Appendixes, page 177) lists late 1968 examples of each type of service given in Table 2-1.

the total market

The total market for information utility services can be broken into the two general types, labelled general purpose (G) and subscriber oriented (S) in column 2 of Table 2-1.

From a market survey or testing point of view, a potential supplier of information utility services could investigate subscriber oriented services by examining one industry or a related group of industries in what might be called a vertical fashion; that is, the market for all information utility services tailored for that industry could be surveyed by staying within the industry. For example, Table 2-1 shows sport and theatre ticket service, which would be sold to agencies and sponsors in the ticket business. Railroad information would be sold to railroads, etc.

The general purpose category, on the other hand, re-

Table 2-1   Types of information utility services

type	general purpose or subscriber oriented	retrieval or processing	digital or graphical
1. Savings account processing	S	P	D
2. Stock brokerage information	S	R	D
3. Travel service	S	P	D
4. Professional billing	S	P	D
5. Engineering problem solving	G	P	D, G
6. Graphical design	G	P	G
7. Document retrieval	G	R	G
8. Data retrieval	G	R	D
9. General purpose	G	P	D, G
10. Credit information	S	R	D
11. Financial exchange–SAVE	Multiple S	P	D
12. Hospital and medical	S	P	D, G
13. Educational and teaching	G, S	P	D, G
14. Hotel reservations	S	P	D
15. Interairline reservations	S	P	D
16. Railroad information	S	P	D
17. Publishing	S	P	D, G
18. Radio and TV time brokerage	S	R	D
19. Retail and distribution	S	P	D
20. Insurance	S	P	D
21. Merchandising and advertising	G	P	D
22. Public survey and polling	G	P	D
23. Sport and theatre tickets	S	P	D
24. Tax service	G	P	D
25. Labor negotiations	S	P	D
26. Career and employment information	G	P	D
27. Legal citation service	S	P	D
28. Post Office	S	P	D
29. Marketing research	G	R	D
30. Criminal intelligence	S	P	D
31. Typing and editing service	G	P	D
32. Personal data services	G	P	D
33. Library catalogs	G	R	D
34. Lottery service	S	P	D

quires that the market for the service be examined horizontally across many industries. Table 2-3 (see Appendixes, page 179) shows a matrix of probable industry users of most of the various services listed in Table 2-1. Only those services usable by more than one industry or type of organization are listed. At each intersection the code indicates whether the service listed is currently (1968) being offered to the type of subscriber (C) or whether it is considered to be a future potential market (P).

type	small, medium, or large subscriber	local, regional, or national
1. Savings account processing	S, M, L	L, R
2. Stock brokerage information	S, M, L	N
3. Travel service	S, M, L	N
4. Professional billing	S	L
5. Engineering problem solving	S, M, L	L, R, N
6. Graphical design	S, M, L	L, R, N
7. Document retrieval	S, M, L	N
8. Data retrieval	S, M, L	L, R, N
9. General purpose	S, M, L	L
10. Credit information	S, M, L	L, R, N
11. Financial exchange–SAVE	S, M, L	L, R, N
12. Hospital and medical	S, M, L	L, R
13. Educational and teaching	S, M, L	L, R, N
14. Hotel reservations	S, M, L	N
15. Interairline reservations	S, M, L	N
16. Railroad information	S, M, L	N
17. Publishing	S, M, L	L, R, N
18. Radio and TV time brokerage	S, M	N
19. Retail and distribution	S, M	L, R
20. Insurance	S, M	L, R
21. Merchandising and advertising	S, M	N
22. Public survey and polling	S	N
23. Sport and theatre tickets	S	L, R, N
24. Tax service	S, M	L
25. Labor negotiations	S, M, L	N
26. Career and employment information	S, M, L	N
27. Legal citation service	S, M, L	N
28. Post Office	L	N
29. Marketing research	M, L	N
30. Criminal intelligence	L	N
31. Typing and editing service	S, M, L	N
32. Personal data services	S	L, R, N
33. Library catalogs	S, M, L	L, R, N
34. Lottery service	M, L	L, R, N

Any study of the total market for all information utility services should include examination of the services marketable to a given industry as well as all of the markets for a given service.

market studies

Since there have been failures of several information utilities, any potential new supplier of utility services should seriously consider a market study prior to entry.

Market studies, particularly in areas, such as time sharing and information utilities, that are affected by new technology, are attended by considerable uncertainty. For any prospective supplier of utility services, the more serious problems that should be explored by studies are the following:

1. Criteria for the selection of promising markets
2. Problems of market entry
3. Appraisal of the determinants of customer acceptance
4. Estimation of market share under competition

The general methodology of a study can be summarized as follows:

1. Outline total market structure (based on Table 2-3).
2. Select markets for initial survey.
3. Conduct preliminary market research by informal interviews with prospective customers for information utility services.
4. Select the most promising markets and services to be further tested.
5. Structure the market for the service, i.e., identification of market use, of individual organizations within the market, and of special characteristics of these organizations.
6. Conduct investigation of the match between the services and the intended market by depth studies with selected potential customers.
7. Measure markets against supplier's capabilities.
8. Make final market selection, including return on investment analysis.

A prerequisite for a statistical market study is a soundly conceived set of services that can be shown or described to the person being interviewed. The market study outline above is aimed at providing the prerequisite and at establishing a first point of reference for management with respect to investment, anticipated cash flow, and rate of return.

This last figure cannot be provided without also undertaking an examination of the following factors:

1. The competitive position for each market for each service

2. The value of each service and hence the pricing structure that will prevail.

3. Resource gaps in supplier's capability for entering market

4. The costs of entering the market.

The fourth factor includes such items as establishing a sales capability and setting up distribution channels.

The four problem areas identified in the first of the preceding lists will be encountered during the examination of these factors. In a sense, the problem areas and the factors are highly interdependent. For example, a large potential market in an area of business unrelated to a potential supplier's current activities implies a high cost of entry and hence a longer development period and a delayed return on investment.

However, a suitable point of departure is to develop criteria for the selection of promising markets. For convenience, these criteria can be separated into those that are a function of the potential information utility supplier's strengths and those that are a function of the market place, including current competition and depth of penetration. The first subgroup would contain criteria derived from consideration of the supplier's financial, physical, managerial, and staffing resources. For example, it is appropriate to determine the general magnitude of the markets that match the supplier's long-term development and to figure the cost of entry that matches the supplier's financial "muscle." The latter requires a consideration not only of "how big is too big" but also of the minimum entry cost to be considered.

A low entry cost means that a promising market can be flooded by small information utilities with low overhead costs, thereby leaving the pioneering supplier with little except the development costs.

The problems of market entry and of customer acceptance are interrelated. Market entry can be difficult because there is either too much competition or too little. In the former case, the problem is one of establishing a "brand" position and will obviously be most severe in those markets in which the supplier's name is unknown. If there is little or no competition, this probably means that customer acceptance will be slow in developing and that the supplier must be prepared to find and support some pilot projects with selected customers.

The following sample of market entry factors is indicative of the complexity of this problem.

1. *Receptivity of markets to traditional versus advanced approaches*, i.e., batch processing versus time sharing, real time, graphics, etc.

2. *Choice of markets:* business or scientific; small/medium/large users; packages or tailored services; machine services only, or consulting and programming as well; "natural" markets, etc.

3. *Organizational problems:* local or national, acquiring companies which already sell IU services, staffing problems, proprietary considerations, selling services, facilities, locations, pricing services, budgets and costs, affiliations (accounting firms, tax consultants, banks, subsidiaries or associated firms of supplier), problems and opportunities presented by existing supplier organization.

The estimation of the potential size of markets has its own problems, such as evaluation of psychological factors, and the detection and appraisal of undeveloped markets with closely related characteristics. For example, in the country's public school systems there is a market for time-shared computing capabilities that bears a close resemblance to the engineering markets. The much larger problem, however, is the estimate of the share-of-the-market that the supplier can hope to gain. The dynamics of this estimate involve forecasting what the competition may do, assessing the probable outcome of counter moves by the supplier, and trying to reduce the estimate to a common denominator in dollars so that decisions can be made. It should be mentioned at this point that, as of early 1969, very few IU owners ever had conducted a market study like the one recommended.

specific examples of early IU's

The earliest IU's were the result of pioneering work in the industries that first made extensive use of on line–real time systems. These included the airlines, savings institutions, hotels, brokerage firms, and stock exchanges. In some cases, a large airline or savings bank, after investing in a system of their own, would begin offering services to subscribers in the same geographic area and in the same business. In other cases, groups of organizations formed and created an IU with joint ownership, offering services to other subscribers as well. The savings banks and savings and loan companies particularly followed this route. Another course of action was followed by organizations in a business directly related to that of a group of institutions opening an IU that is based on initially signing up a certain minimum number of customers. Again, savings institution services actively pursued this course, with commercial banks and bank trust companies being the IU owners.

savings account IU

The savings account processing type of IU merits some discussion because of its early development and because it is characteristic of a service oriented toward a particular industry and application. There are in operation, consequently, more of this type than almost any type.

The savings account processing service provides subscribing savings banks or savings and loan associations with a complete account recording and updating for all savings accounts. The service is supplied at tellers' windows on the floor of all branches of the subscriber institution by means of specially designed teller terminals, or window machines as they are popularly labelled. (See Figure 2-1.) A teller at any window is able to process a customer completely, including deposits, withdrawals, special conditions, interest calculations, and posting of the passbook. The time taken to process a customer is reduced from the level required by manual or off-line computer systems. This type of system, while developed by large savings institutions, brings to even the smallest savings and loan association, through the utility concept, an economical service comparable to the best the large institutions have to offer.

The central computer programs are relatively fixed, so

Figure 2-1   Savings bank window terminal. (Courtesy National Cash Register Corporation)

that savings institution subscribers do no programming or systems design work. Several preprogrammed options are usually made available for each part of the service. For example, a selection would be offered of methods of computing interest, or of types of holds and methods for placing the holds from certain terminals.

The service also usually includes processing of loans or mortgages, Christmas Club and other special types of savings accounts, and many other services, some of which are provided in an off-line mode.

Perhaps the best known example of a savings institution IU is the one operated and owned by the Savings and Loan Bank of New York. In this case, a bank, which is owned by the savings and loan associations in New York State and which provides services for all state S & L's, became the owner and operator of the IU. The subscribing institutions are primarily the smaller savings and loan associations in the state, although any customer of the central bank is eligible. The service has been in operation since 1966.

In the mid-1960's, OLRT savings account systems moved from the experimental pioneering state into full-scale production. Nearly every small savings bank or savings and loan association in the United States has had an opportunity to become a subscriber to a nearby savings account service or to share in the operation of one. Areas in which savings utility services are now (1969) offered include: New York, Chicago, Boston, Cleveland, St. Louis, Los Angeles, Rochester, Tacoma, Minneapolis, Buffalo, Newark, New Haven, Miami, Detroit, Spokane, Wilmington, Beverly Hills, Glendale, Phoenix, New Orleans, Fort Lauderdale, Queens, Pittsburgh, Brooklyn, Illinois, Indiana, Iowa, Connecticut, and Westchester County.

In Rochester, New York, Pittsburgh, Detroit and several of the other cities, groups of savings institutions banded together to attempt the formation of a shared ownership arrangement. In Boston, New York, Los Angeles, Chicago, Fort Lauderdale, and several other cities, National Cash Register or Burroughs Corporation own the utility.

In Boston, the Provident Institute for Savings is an example of a large savings institution that started its own service and signed up smaller subscribers at a later time. In Chicago, Continental, a commercial bank, sells savings services to savings institutions as well as to other commercial banks. In St. Louis, the Bank of St. Louis does the same thing.

stockbroker services

A second type of utility representative of the single industry orientation is the stock brokerage information utility.

Three nationwide stock brokerage information utilities have been operating for several years. They are Telequote (a Bunker-Ramo–Teleregister Division service), Quotron (a Scantlin Electronics Corporation service), and Stockmaster (an Ultronics Corporation service). A fourth service was initiated in 1968 for the block transaction market. It is called AutEx and operates primarily in New York.

The first three IU's provide brokers in all parts of the country with up-to-the-second information on stock market transactions, market trends and averages, and various other market data. In recent years, all three have expanded their services to include the processing of brokers' buy-sell orders, investors' accounts, portfolio and market analysis, and other associated functions.

Initially, the brokerage services displayed stock transaction prices on large boards in brokers' offices. This nationwide service was actually started in 1929 by the Teleregister Corporation, using electrical and electromechanical techniques. It utilized digital data transmission, however, and was probably the first national information utility. The emergence of Quotron and Stockmaster led to both computers and digital querying types of displays.

With the latter, the broker keys in the identity of the stock his customer is asking about and a code for the type of information he wants, i.e., last price, bid and asked prices, the open, high, and low for the day, volume, trend, etc. He receives a reply in a second or two either in the form of a

Figure 2-2   Telequote 70 brokerage service terminal. (Courtesy Bunker Ramo Corporation)

printed response or a display on a cathode ray tube or small electronic indicators. (See Figure 2-2.) The customer's man is thus able to answer questions quickly at his desk while the customer is on the phone.

In New York, the broker may also hear the response on his phone through computer generated voice replies. This service is part of special New York information utilities operated by both the New York Stock Exchange and the American Stock Exchange for brokers in the metropolitan area. The stock identity and transaction information codes are dialed on the broker's own telephone, thus eliminating the need for a special terminal.

In fact, there are strong indications that both stock exchanges may become owners of very large information utilities supplementing and perhaps competing with the existing three utilities.

Another utility in the formative stages for the over-the-counter market is NASDAQ, announced publicly by Bunker

Ramo Corporation. It will provide the same type of query and display services for unlisted stocks as the three national utilities provide for listed stocks. Another utility, AutEx, will provide block stock information simultaneously to all subscribers. The over-the-counter brokerage market will also be served by this utility. When an institution wants to sell a large block, brokers can actually place their order for part of it through the AutEx CRT on their desk.

travel service

The travel service utility is included as an example of a type determined more by the industry than by the kinds of subscribers, of which there are a wide variety. The subscribers for travel service could be travel agents, airlines, shipping lines, railroads, car rental agencies, hotels, motels, and resorts.

The services would include availability information for lodging accommodations and for all modes of transport sold by the subscribers listed above, listing of space for sale, booking and confirmation service, including notification of travel company or hotel selling the space, and inventory control of space being sold.

The big advantage of such a utility for both subscribers and travellers is that a multiple segment itinerary can be booked all at one time with reservation confirmations on all space. The traveller, while on the phone or standing at a ticket counter or sitting at a travel agent's desk, is assured of reservations immediately for all parts of his trip, including his hotels and motels. The travel agent, using a single terminal connected to the travel utility (see Figure 2-3), can book the space on airlines, railroads, steamships, rental cars, hotels, or resorts. He does not have to make separate phone calls or send telegrams or write letters to each of the organizations involved in an itinerary. Furthermore, neither he nor his client have to wait days or weeks for all of the replies to come back with their attendant rejects or suggested alternatives. If the hotel room or airline flight desired

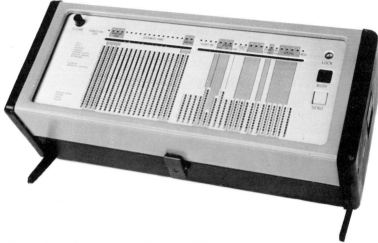

Figure 2-3 Travel service terminal. (Courtesy Telemax Corporation, Fairfield, New Jersey)

by the traveller is not available, alternates are immediately shown on the terminal display for selection by the customer.

There are actually two types of subscribers for the travel service. The first is a travel agent or other agency making the trip arrangements for travellers. The second is an organization, like an airline or a hotel, that has space for sale. The service charges for the first type are based on a per transaction rate, which would vary as a function of the type of space being sold. Charges for the second type are based on a monthly rate, which is dependent on the amount and type of space listed for sale. Several variations on this type of service charge would be possible, ranging from listing availability only, with bookings to be transacted in some other manner, up to complete inventory control of space.

It is possible for one organization to subscribe to both types of services. For example, an airline or a railroad could list its own space and also sell space on other airlines, railroads, or hotels.

In practice, those companies who have their own reservations systems will probably become subscribers only to the first type of service. The inventory control of hotel rooms for Sheraton and of airline seats for American and United Airlines, for example, will continue to be performed in their own systems. However, there may be electronic links between these systems and the various travel information utilities, so that availability status resulting from changes in inventory can be posted in the utility center. Conversely, bookings coming from travel agents through the utilities can be passed on automatically to the individual reservation systems.

There are currently (1968) two leading contenders for nationwide travel services. They are Telemax Corporation and General Data Corporation, a subsidiary of Holiday Inns, Inc. The Telemax service was proposed to travel agents and various travel companies in 1964 with the intention of starting the service whenever a sufficient number of advance subscriptions were obtained. It was proposed as a full-scale national service like the type described above.

General Data Corporation was formed to offer hotel and motel reservations services based on the already existing nationwide system for Holiday Inns room reservations. Recently, General Data has announced a series of utility services that could lead to the travel service described.

Earlier, Teleregister Corporation had proposed a travel service, but it was withdrawn from the market. Ticket Reservations Service has indicated its possible entrance into the travel service markets. ATARS already links together all the airlines; hence, it can obviously be tied into any viable travel service. Control Data Corporation also offers SAFIR to travel agents for airline reservations, and is planning to offer a travel service.

professional billing service

Professional billing service for doctors, dentists, lawyers, clinics, and medical centers is an example of an information utility servicing very small businesses. In fact, the service can be provided to a single doctor, although it has been sold primarily to groups located in centers.

The basic idea is that the doctor and his nurses or other assistants can be relieved of the paperwork involved in making out bills and in collecting receivables. The telephone plays an important part in this service. The doctor is supplied by the utility with sets of punched cards, one for each patient and one for each type of treatment.

After each patient has been treated, the doctor or his nurse dials the number of the utility and then inserts a card identifying the patient and another identifying the treatment into a card reading device attached to the telephone. The dataphone combination transmits the information to the utility where the customer's account is updated. This may be done off line or on line. The utility then sends each patient a bill at the end of the proper period. Depending on the agreement between the utility and the doctor, payment by the patient is sent either to the doctor or to the utility. An intermediate arrangement can be made by which the payments are sent to a post office box, which the patient thinks is the doctor's, although it is actually the utility's. As far as the doctor and his nurses are concerned in the latter two arrangements, they are through with the transaction and all paper work or collecting worries just as soon as the dataphone transmission takes place.

If the treatments are not simple enough to be easily identified by prepunched cards, or in the event a patient with no card is treated, provision for keyboard entry of the required data can be made. Either touch tone or dialing numerical codes can be done, or a simple keyboard can be attached to the phone. Alternatively, the utility center can be called by phone, and keying in can be done there by an operator.

The professional billing service may possibly eliminate the need for certain clerical personnel, particularly in a large medical center where many doctors and dentists can share an input telephone station.

The best known example of a professional billing service is MEDAC, a franchised service initiated by a group in Milwaukee, Wisconsin. MEDAC has been offered by several banks and private companies around the country. It has been copied by many others. This type of service has now become available in nearly every major city in the United States.

hospital utilities

Three different technological developments have begun to merge in the hospital and medical fields to produce information utilities for doctors, hospitals, and medical centers.

The earliest advance was the design of on line–real time systems for hotel and hospital room reservations and patient or guest accounting and billing. Developments in these areas in hotel reservation systems are almost directly applicable to hospitals even though several years elapsed between the emergence of the first hotel reservation systems and the application to the hospitals. The second area of research has been the application of computer time sharing to medical diagnosis. The third area has been the use of on-line instrumentation and monitoring techniques coupled to computers to determine a patient's condition on a real time basis. These three developments have now been brought together; first, to serve a single hospital; and, secondly, in a utility form serving many hospitals in a community or a larger geographical area.

In both cases, the concept involves a large-scale central computer storing on line all patient treatment information on a historical basis, all current patient treatment data, selected patient real time monitoring information, room and service availability, records of room and service usage, and medical research data of various types.

On-line terminals in the hospitals are of several types (see title page illustration and Figure 2-4). For reservation and billing functions, the registration desks, cashier checkout stations, nurses' stations, laboratories, meal service areas, telephone desk, medical supplies stations and doctor

Figure 2-4   Digiscribe hospital terminal.
(Courtesy Control Data Corporation)

locations are all equipped with data terminals. An inventory of rooms is maintained. A reservations function is performed. Patient check-in is recorded. Patient charges for all services are recorded, and patient check-out plus billing is handled in an on-line fashion. The laboratories and selected emergency patient areas are also equipped with on-line measuring devices that can be fastened to patients.

The service in its totality will free doctors, nurses, laboratory personnel, and others from the routine data gathering, data processing, record handling, and statistical research that now take up much of their time. It will also provide a valuable man-machine approach to medical diagnosis, treatment and research. It will streamline and coordinate more efficiently the maintenance of all records concerned with an individual patient as well as produce more up-to-date and accurate information on the availability of rooms and services. Since more than 50 per cent of the hospital beds in the United States are in hospitals with fewer than 200 beds, an information utility approach seems essential.

As an example of the type of patient record-doctor diagnosis use that might be made of a hospital information utility, take a new patient entering with pneumonia and ulcers. Today, the doctor cannot answer some key questions such as: "What happened to the last 25 patients who had pneumonia and ulcers at the same time? Was drug x prescribed for any of them? If so, did it help them in any way?"

However, with an IU, the doctor, while treating a patient or making a diagnosis, can be aided and guided in a series of steps by the conversational mode through his terminal at the patient's own location or in his office. For example, the utility prints out the time and date and asks the doctor to identify himself for the record, which he does. Hospital identity is derived automatically from the location of the terminal. The doctor identifies the patient by number, and the service corroborates it by typing the patient's name and other data on file.

The utility then requests the medication being prescribed. As each item is specified by the doctor, the system questions any errors. The service may also question the particular drug or quantity after checking it against the patient's past history. The doctor either confirms his specification, or delves into why there should be a question by asking the service for its records. He may then decide to change the prescription. After the conversation is complete, the utility prints back the corrected treatment order in full. The doctor signs it by entering his code, and the order is then made part of the patient's record, while printed outputs at nurses' stations and supply stations trigger off follow-up actions.

There are obviously many psychological and sociological implications in the hospital utility concept described. The doctors, nurses, patients, and administrative staffs will have to accept new ideas. The barrier of the psychological feeling that automation should not interfere with professional work or opinion must be overcome before this type of utility will come into widespread use. Yet, there are signs that these new concepts are being, and will be, accepted.

The leading research in hospital time sharing has taken place at the Massachusetts General Hospital and at the Boston firm of Bolt Beranek and Newman. A joint project set up an experimental time sharing facility for the one hospital. However, a second major goal of the project was formation of a utility to serve a number of hospitals in the community. On a national basis, General Electric Company has been marketing the system developed by this project, using the name Medinet.

A group of hospitals and Minnesota Blue Cross in Minneapolis and St. Paul placed in operation a hospital information utility utilizing computer equipment supplied by Minneapolis Honeywell. Eight hospitals became joint participants in the service, and 170 were potential subscribers. This service has been offered on a nationwide basis by Honeywell.

The Veterans Administration has been conducting research in on-line patient monitoring and medical diagnosis for several years. A program to put VA hospitals on line is in the planning stage. Children's Hospital of Boston has had a patient monitoring system in operation for some time, although no plans have been announced to convert it into a utility. However, the Philadelphia General Hospital has already planned for the use of an on line–real time system. A group of hospitals in Indianapolis subscribe to a utility service, Indianapolis Hospital Development Association, that is offered by a separate corporation but financed by all of them.

information retrieval utilities

One broad class of information utilities may be described as the information retrieval type. The words "information retrieval" have taken on several meanings to various groups in the data processing, library, and professional society areas. In general, they mean placing information in a file and retrieving it again. The variations in meaning are a function of the form in which the information is stored and the techniques for identifying, indexing, and retrieving it.

To most laymen, the form of storage implied is visual, whether it be printed or filmed. To some professionals, the words imply electronic or magnetic forms of storage. To still other specialists, an information retrieval system is primarily the special techniques for coding and indexing the information so that it can be retrieved in a variety of ways.

Information retrieval utilities in the context of this book will be taken to mean any service that has the utility characteristics described in Chapter 1, and that stores information and later retrieves it without modification or processing. In other words, the prime function of such a utility is to allow users to put information away and later retrieve it again.

The form of storage can be electronic, magnetic, printed, photographic, or microfilm. The methods of indexing, coding, and retrieving can vary widely. The form of output may be the same as the form of storage, for example, both microfilm; or it may be different, for example, magnetic storage and printed output.

Two different types of information retrieval utilities seem to be emerging. The first type merely provides storage space and input-output facilities at remote terminals. The subscriber stores away his own information in an allocated space and can retrieve it later. This method is analogous to a personal filing system. The second type involves information being collected from many sources, all of which is made available to any subscriber. This method is analogous to a library system.

Retrievals may be made of individual items separately identified or of groups of items all meeting a specific set of criteria. In both cases, the on-line nature of the utility is advantageous in the retrieval process, because the service can aid, guide, instruct, and remind the subscriber how the information he seeks was filed originally and therefore help

Figure 2-5   Legal citation service terminal.
(Courtesy Law Research Corporation)

him find it. Much of the laborious file searching, cross-index searching, and reference trail work now engaged in by information retrievers working with nonutility libraries or files will be done by the utility service itself. Again, the conversational mode of operation, in which the utility "talks to" the subscriber and vice versa, is essential in shortening the searching process.

Lawyers expect to save hours and perhaps days in legal research, brief preparation, and court strategy by gaining access to legal history through the use of utility techniques. (See Figure 2-5.) The patent office hopes to reduce substantially the present long delays in the processing and issuing of patents. Trademark and copyright searchers would benefit in the same way. Engineers hope to reduce the time required in exploring prior research and development work in the field of a new endeavor. The usual expression of this desire is "Let's not reinvent the wheel over and over again, just because we do not know it has been invented." In the chemical field, thousands of new compounds are discovered or created every day. With a central information retrieval utility, it will be feasible for a chemical engineer or scientist to inquire today about all of the new compounds related to his work that have been created up to the past day or even hour.

The *personal file* type of utility is represented by Personal Data Services, a service that may be offered on a nationwide basis.[1] It will provide for entry of information from a variety of terminals at subscriber locations in most major US cities and will supply storage in electronic-magnetic form for later retrieval by the subscriber who entered the information. The terminals to be available are CRT's with light pens.

Many examples of the *library* type of information retrieval utility have been under development. The earliest organizations working on such projects were the various professional groups in the fields of chemistry, physics, and law. Federal government agencies as well as libraries and librarians also took an early interest.

The current examples of actual operating utilities are very small in number. However, several government operated services are in the planning stages. The prime interest in them is the availability at remote locations of technical and scientific information from one library type of center.

The Department of Defense, the National Institute of Health, the Patent Office, the National Science Foundation, the Clearinghouse for Scientific and Technical Information, the Library of Congress, the National Bureau of Standards, the National Academy of Science, and Chemical Abstracts Service are all interested in either sponsoring or subscribing to information retrieval utilities.

Within professional groups, several law societies and

1. The concept of PDS will be described in a book now in preparation by the author. See also Chapter 6.

groups, the American Society of Chemical Engineers, the Institute of Electronic and Electrical Engineers, the National Academy of Engineering, the Engineers Joint Council, and various medical associations are interested. The University of Pittsburgh and Tulane University have proposed setting up national information retrieval utilities for technical and scientific information to service university libraries, government agencies, and professional groups.

A few university libraries, notably Florida Atlantic University, University of Illinois, and the University of Michigan, have been developing information utilities to serve students and professors on the campus. The retrieval schemes permit reference search work at points throughout the campus, with later retrieval in the library of the actual volumes or documents, either in original form or on microfilm.

It is probable that this form of information utility will continue to emerge on a national basis with nonprofit government or professional sponsorship. The library type of information needs tends to be universal, and the IU's serving them will be of greater value if they can be constituted on a nationwide scale.

part ii   *examples*

This chapter and the next five chapters will describe in more detail six widely divergent information utilities. The information revolution predicted in the opening section of the book and the impact of information utilities on each of us as individuals will become more apparent from these six chapters.

The impact of the general purpose and problem solving (time sharing) types of utilities has already been felt by engineers, scientists, operations researchers, students, and other technically oriented individuals. The minds and ways of thought and learning of these people have already begun to undergo fundamental changes. For this reason it is important to examine these two types of utilities in detail.

3 general purpose problem solving utility

the general purpose information utility

The first general purpose information utilities in the United States began operation in the late 1960's. Entrepreneurs in local areas had already announced plans for general purpose utilities as early as 1965. Keydata, Western Union, IT&T, GE, CEIR, CDC, SBC, Ultronics, and others indicated national intentions.

What is the difference between the *time sharing* or engineering problem solving type of utility and the *general purpose* utility? Can the former evolve into the latter? This chapter will examine some of the technical and marketing differences and will describe a general purpose type in some detail.

A general purpose information utility, as the name implies, is set up to provide services to many different kinds of subscribers. It supplies both fixed packaged programmed services and general program and storage capabilities. Engineering problem solving, information retrieval, graphical design, and a variety of business and accounting services are included in its "product" lines.

For the general purpose utility, a number of system design and marketing problems exist that can be avoided in the more limited service types. These problems will be discussed in more detail in Chapter 9. They stem from two sources. The first has to do with the security and protection of stored information. When both programming and non-programming subscribers begin to share the utility's files, some special steps must be taken to prevent file disturbance and unauthorized access.

The second source of problems has to do with the way services for nonprogramming business subscribers are added to the utility and the way they are priced and marketed. As long as a utility sticks to one type of service for

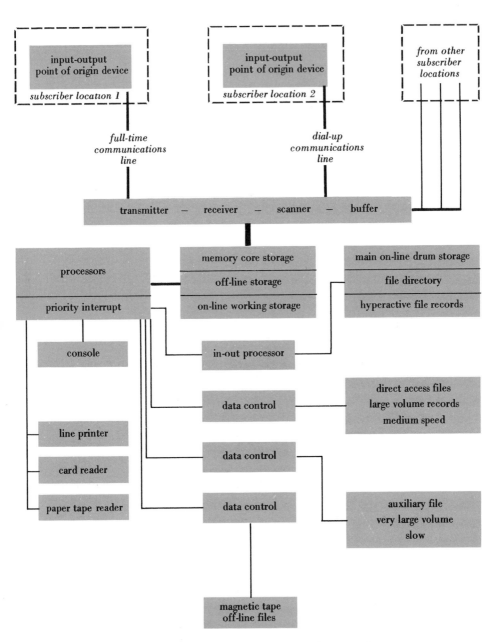

Figure 3-1   Diagram of general purpose information utility (based on Keydata Corporation system).

one class of subscribers (savings account processing, for example), a limited number of variations in the service will satisfy most subscribers. As the variety of subscribers and services increases, the problems of constructing the packaged program, of pricing unrelated services, and of tailoring the services to meet the demands of a wide variety of types of subscribers multiply rapidly.

The general purpose utility is then faced with a series of system and marketing decisions, interwoven with financial investment problems. One approach is to begin with the programming type subscribers, selling primarily computational or processing capability plus file space. After a utility base has been assembled, simple packaged program services might then be added.

A second approach is to start on the nonprogramming package side and offer to small subscribers those business services that are common to as many small businesses as possible. Accounting services or tax services are good possibilities, since all small businesses must be concerned with them. Keydata has utilized this approach and has selected the accounting functions of customer billing, accounts receivable, and inventory control for subscribers in the distribution business as the initial base package service on which to build.

Whichever growth approach is used, the systems problems can become traps unless the information utility plans for growth in terms of hardware, software, and especially control techniques.

Figure 3-1 shows the various hardware elements in one particular general purpose utility. Above the horizontal bar are the input-output devices (POD's) at points of origin in subscriber locations. Two types of communications links from the POD's to the utility center are shown. On the left, subscriber number one has his own leased full-time line. In the center, subscriber number two dials a connection via the public telephone network. He retains the on-line connection for varying amounts of time, ranging from one transaction time to perhaps all day. The lines or dial-up connections from all subscribers are scanned by central communications equipment containing transmitting and receiving facilities, buffer storage, and electronic scanning capabilities.

Below the communications equipment bar is the rest of the hardware at the central utility location. There will probably be at least two multiprocessors, which are capable of simultaneous processing with shared storage, and perhaps more. This particular IU utilizes a separate processor to control input and output actions among the main processor's interrupt system, the fast working storage, and the main on-line drum storage. Input from and output to the central communications buffers is directly from the fast core storage.

Four levels of storage are used in a hierarchical fashion, so that information needed most rapidly is obtained from core, the fastest level. Programs, file directories, and hyperactive file records are in drum storage, the second level, and surged into core when needed. The third level of storage is made up of direct access disc files for medium speed, large volume records, and is under a separate data control. The fourth level is an auxiliary file for very large volume requirements, also under separate control. This file is still on line, although its access time may be considerably longer. During the foreseeable near future, it will probably be a tape strip or magnetic card file.

In addition, there is the usual complement of off-line equipment, such as card reader and punch, line printer, paper tape or optical scanning reader, and magnetic tape units.

During a working day the location of any single file or record may be dynamically changed from one level of storage to another. An index or chain is maintained, so that the *system* knows where the record is, even though the subscriber does not. File activity is monitored, so that more frequently accessed information moves up toward core level, while that needed less frequently moves down toward auxiliary file level. Each lower level of storage acts as backup for the one above it in the event of hardware failure. Subscriber programs are kept mainly in drum storage, while the overall control, or executive, program is kept in core.

The system design described here allows expansion for additional subscribers, new applications, more storage, greater processing capability, and subscriber locations at any point where communications costs can be justified. It should also be possible to begin with less than the hardware in Figure 3-1 and grow from a time-shared problem solving utility to the general purpose type.

An executive program monitors and controls all activity within the system and handles selection indexing and record keeping of file locations. All programs are executed in interpreted mode under executive program control. Therefore, a subscriber writing and checking programs from his terminal is unable to use or "get at" machine language instructions. This factor is very important for program and file protection against programmer errors as well as machine failures. Chapter 9 will enlarge on this point.

A system of passwords combined with communication techniques is used to prevent subscribers from obtaining access to each other's records and to create levels of authorization for inquiry to or changing of records by various classes of individuals.

problem solving utility

The time sharing services and systems that have been given so much publicity are really the general purpose utility in its infancy. Most time sharing utilities are used by individuals with at least some basic knowledge of programming. Problems are solved in a new way using interactive techniques, and yet a type of programming is actually accomplished. The programming language may be relatively simple and easily understood, as in GE's BASIC or Rand Corporation's JOSS. Nevertheless, programming is used in the problem solving techniques. The individual user is instructing the service in how to help him solve his problem.

The subscribers may be engineers, scientists, operations researchers, management scientists, economists, or even accountants. They may become subscribers as individuals or as members of a group, a task force, or a problem solving team. Problem solving is really too limited a description of this type of utility. The engineer may be designing a product or the scientist may be using simulation techniques or the economist may be constructing a mathematical model. The common characteristic of all uses of this type of utility is man–machine communication, or dialogue, as some have labeled it. (See Figure 3-2.)

The subscriber is, in effect, in constant conversation back and forth with the equivalent of his own computer. He can set up his own files in the computer and can develop his own problem solving formulas or techniques. In most versions of the problem solving utility, the subscriber can prepare his own programs and test (or debug) them from his own terminal. There are certain versions in which this procedure cannot be followed, where the subscriber must use a set of standard programs available to him. If he needs a new program, it is necessary in these cases to have the utility's staff test the programs at the computer center.

The programming or problem solving languages used by subscribers range from scientifically oriented languages such as Fortran and Algol, to user oriented languages such as JOSS.[1] The English language end of the range allows a subscriber to converse with the utility without ever really knowing that computer programs exist or that each step in his problem solving technique involves execution of computer subroutines. In the most sophisticated utilities, an analytical solution to a complex mathematically expressed problem can be arrived at by creating a succession of analytical functions. These functions are created by a combination of button pushing and light pen tracing on a cathode ray tube. The functional meaning of a particular button on the keyboard can be changed and stored at the option of

1. JOSS is a user oriented language developed at Rand Corporation.

Figure 3-2   Teletype terminal. (Courtesy General Electric Company Time Sharing Services)

the user. Thus, the language used can be called, "Button Pushing and Interpretation."

The advantages of this type of service to the individual engineer can be summed up by saying that he has the equivalent of his own large-scale computer right next to his desk, but he does not have to know much about computers or computer programming to use it. He or his firm pay only for the amount of use, and so this service can be very economical.

This type of information utility received much of its impetus on university campuses and other nonprofit research organizations. The Advanced Research Projects Agency (ARPA) of the Department of Defense supported several of the early developments. ARPA sponsored pioneering projects at Rand Corporation (The JOSS Service), System Development Corporation, MIT (Project MAC), and the University of Utah. More recently, Dartmouth, Carnegie Institute of Technology, University of Michigan, and others have opened time sharing centers. Computer manufacturers entered the field in 1965 with the announcements of utility services by GE, IBM, Control Data Corporation, and Scientific Data Systems in cooperation with the University of California at Berkeley. At least one industrial concern (Socony Mobil Oil Company) had, as early as 1964, put into operation a worldwide utility for the use of its engineers and scientists.

Service bureaus and software firms also opened centers or announced plans. Among them were CEIR and Computer Sciences Corporation. Data communications companies, notably IT&T and Western Union, also got into the act in 1965 by announcing their intentions to provide engineering time sharing services. Finally, various private entrepreneurs have started problem solving utilities and services in several communities around the country. University Computing of Dallas and Applied Logic Corporation of Princeton are examples.

The proliferation of problem solving time sharing services is illustrated by the lists in Tables 3-1, 3-2, and 3-3, reproduced from pamphlets published by Computer Research Corporation, Newton, Massachusetts, and Time Sharing Enterprises, Inc. (For Tables 3-1, 3-2, and 3-3, see Appendixes, pages 184–192.)

graphical design information utility

A utility whose characteristics are similar to the engineering problem solving type is the graphical design information utility. The service provided to engineers, architects, scientists, and other designers by this type of utility is difficult to classify. Its purpose is to facilitate design of products, structures, and other things in which graphical or drafting-drawing techniques are usually used.

The user, utilizing a terminal equipped with graphical

display facilities, is in constant conversational mode with the service. (See Figure 3-3.) A light pen or similiar electronic drawing device is used to put in graphical information. The designer uses techniques that are quite similar to those used in the problem solving case, except that the information exchange mode is primarily graphical in nature. The net result of the user's efforts is a product design that is stored in both digital and graphical form in the utility's memory and can be printed or sketched or displayed in either form for the user.

The designer, in entering graphical information, does not have to be an accurate draftsman. He can, for example, specify that a straight line be drawn between two points. First, he either presses a key or touches with a light pen a button or a particular position on the display screen. This action inserts the code for straight line. Then he draws a roughly straight line between the two points. He can specify the points again by touching the screen or by keying in their coordinates.

A host of graphical shapes and symbols can be displayed for him by the system. He can choose one by light pen pointing, say a circle, move it to some selected point on the screen with the pen, enlarge its radius or shrink it, draw spokes in it, rotate it, etc. By combining shapes and moving, rotating, and adjusting sizes, the designer can draw nearly anything imaginable. The accuracy of the dimensions and positions, sizes and shapes of lines can be specified mathematically and stored if necessary in digital form to achieve the desired accuracy.

It is immediately obvious that the impact of this type of utility on the entire design procedure is substantial. A designer need no longer wait until his first stage sketches have been turned into mechanical drawings and fed back to him in several hours or days. The effect on drafting and draftsmen will also be substantial. The combination of computation, problem solving, and graphical design is potentially powerful in opening entirely new vistas for designers.

Several research projects simultaneously produced workable graphical design systems in 1964 and 1965. Utilities offering services of this type were just beginning to appear in 1966. General Motors and IBM jointly developed a system called DAC 1. MIT, with sponsorship from ARPA, introduced Sketchpad. Itek Corporation developed a service with the

Figure 3-3   Graphical design terminal. (Courtesy Information Display, Incorporated)

help of Adams Associates. Bunker-Ramo produced a series of graphical input-output devices and consoles and new techniques for using them in the graphical design process. Digital Equipment Corporation developed Graphpad. Rand Corporation offered GRAIL (Graphic Input Language). Philco introduced Graphden and Tacden.

Some of the engineering problem solving utilities listed earlier have also announced their intention to offer graphical design services, utilizing one or more of the systems and input-output devices listed previously. IBM will make graphical design services, based on the DAC 1 project, available from several utility centers. (See also Table 3-1.)

4 system for automatic value exchange (save)

status

The information utilities that will have the greatest impact on business and on our society in general are those in which information common to a variety of types of subscribers is not only stored but also exchanged among them. The most significant utility of this type that has been proposed for the future is a *system for automatic value exchange*, with the acronym SAVE.

The word "value" is taken to mean information concerning the value of goods or services. It encompasses all of the forms of representation of value, including cash, checks, money orders, letters of credit, invoices, credit cards, bills, etc.

The word "exchange" means an exchange or transfer of value between two parties or two accounts, whether individuals or organizations.

The word "automatic" is taken, in this context, to mean an electronically mechanized transfer of value from one account to another, at a time close to the actual transaction involving the exchange of goods or services.

"System" means either a local, regional, or national system for accomplishing these automatic exchanges of value.

Other terms which have been used as synonyms for SAVE are "funds transfer," "payment systems," and the "payment mechanism."

Actually, the idea of substituting electronic transmission of information about value for checks or money orders is not new. However, until the technology developed to the state that it reached in the mid-1960's, the idea fell into the "blue sky" category. Now the technology exists, so that construction of the system can begin. In fact, most of the pieces of it have already been implemented by one type of organization or another, but not all of them have been brought together by any one organization.

example of operation

To explain SAVE, a hypothetical example will be given of a consumer making a purchase in a metropolitan area where a SAVE center is in operation. Mr. Jack Smith enters the appliance department of Universal Retail Stores, Inc., to buy a vacuum cleaner selling for $53.00. After Jack and the sales girl have selected the cleaner and agreed on the purchase, Jack presents his SAVE card to the girl. This is a plastic card with Jack's personal identity number encoded on it. It has replaced all of his other local credit cards and most of his national credit cards. It has also replaced all but a small amount of cash or traveler's checks, which he used to carry. It is *not* a credit card. It merely identifies Jack to the system.

The sales girl inserts the card into a slot in a device on the counter called a transactor or terminal or point of origin device. The terminal at Universal Retail is connected directly to the SAVE center in town by a communications line or service. The terminal has replaced the cash register that was formerly on the counter.

Next, the girl inserts a sales slip into another position in the terminal and pushes a key labeled "Start." The number on Jack's SAVE card is transmitted to the center where a computer looks in a file, withdraws identification data about Jack, converts it automatically into voice signals, and sends it back to the telephone on the counter next to the terminal. The sales girl hears over the phone, "Verify: Jack Smith, 1421 Adam Avenue, age 40, blue eyes, red hair, 5'11", 176 pounds."

If the computerized description does not match, the sales girl may take some action as instructed by her boss. If it does match, she presses a key labeled "Verify," and the SAVE center responds with "Enter transaction type" over the phone. She presses a key marked "Sale," and the response is "Enter purchase price." She enters the amount of $53.00 on a ten-button keyboard, and the computer responds with "Amount $53.00." As a further check, the terminal can also display the amount for the customer.

At this point, the system makes several decisions. First, Jack Smith's SAVE records are checked to see whether he is delinquent in payments being made to SAVE or whether the $53.00 will make his balance go negative. If neither of these conditions is true, the system says to the sales girl "Purchase authorized." The terminal then prints the transaction on the sales slip and ejects it, so that the girl can hand Jack Smith his copy after he has signed it. Another copy can be retained if desired for auditing purchases.

At this exact moment, when the printout occurs, an exchange of value of $53.00 takes place between Jack Smith's account and Universal Retail, Inc. Assuming that both accounts are stored in the SAVE center, or in bank systems tied on line to the SAVE center, the exchange is reflected immediately in their respective accounts records.

If Jack is nondelinquent but the purchase sends his balance negative, SAVE will automatically inject a predetermined sum of money into his account from a lending pool supplied by participating banks. This may, for example, be $50 or $100. Jack's bank will be automatically signaled, and three entries will be made in Jack's account record: one, a debit of $53.00 in his value account; two, an injection of credit of $50 or $100 in the value account; and three, a debit of $50 or $100 in his SAVE loan account. If Jack repays the $50 or $100 within a specified interest free period (for example, 30 to 45 days), he will be charged no interest. If he does not, SAVE will charge him the prespecified interest rate, which is comparable to that charged by stores on revolving accounts.

The third possibility is that Jack may be both below zero with this purchase and delinquent on past payments or have something else wrong with his record. In this case, the system automatically displays Jack's record to an authorizer in the center and connects the sales girl to the authorizer's telephone. A conversation may then clear up the situation, and the authorizer may decide to OK the purchase, entering the decision and reason for it on the sales terminal. The transaction then proceeds as before.

If a negative decision is reached, Jack can be informed about why it was reached and may take corrective action or appeal to the nearest SAVE office in person or by phone. Universal Retail is out of the picture altogether. If the purchase is authorized, Universal gets their money immediately, and SAVE takes the responsibility for collecting and credit injection plus interest due. If the transaction is rejected, SAVE is the organization doing the rejecting, not Universal.

overall objectives of save

This example, so far, has illustrated three of SAVE's basic services: purchase authorization, value exchange for goods purchased at a point of sale, and revolving overdraft credit extension. There are many other services in the SAVE concept, and these are listed in Table 4-1. Before we continue

Table 4-1   Types of transactions in a credit and financial utility (SAVE)

---

1. Authorize purchase on credit.
2. Record and bill credit purchases.
3. Authorize cashing of check.
4. Authorize opening of new charge account.
5. Establish demand deposit account.
6. Establish credit utility account.
7. Process check against DDA.
8. Inject funds into credit account.
9. Automatically transfer funds from one DDA account to another.
10. Automatically transfer funds from DDA account to credit account.
11. Automatically transfer funds from corporate account to payroll DDA accounts.
12. Automatically transfer fixed amount every month between DDA accounts.
13. Transfer authorized amount not to exceed specified maximum per instruction from payee.
14. Transfer authorized amounts from DDA account to other utility subscriber accounts up to specified maximum.
15. Establish periodic budget for most expenditures and control DDA and credit accounts within budget.

---

with the example of Jack Smith and describe the other services, it seems desirable to examine the overall objectives of the concept.

Martin Greenberger of Project MAC at MIT told the banking fraternity that "money is information."[1] Looked at from his point of view, money and anything else used to represent value can be replaced by electronic transmissions or magnetic records, thus eliminating the need for checks, cash, money orders, bills, etc.

The elimination of money is the core feature of SAVE. The growing abstraction of value, which began with barter, extended to currency having some intrinsic value like beads or gold coins, evolved to base metals like the Chinese money tree, then to paper currency, and finally to money orders, traveler's checks, and credit cards, should continue and not stop. With SAVE the progression will continue, although the trend toward all transactions being credit transactions would be reversed. The really basic new idea in the SAVE concept is that most transactions will be essentially cash transactions. Under SAVE, payment for goods and services and the exchange of value for them between supplier and consumer will take place as near to the actual time of exchange of the goods and services themselves as possible. The exchange will take place as the first rather than the last step in the normal value clearing and settlement process.

Today, actual collection of value, even without any interest charges, involves several steps, from provision of goods or services through accounting, then billing, check writing, check mailing and handling, possibly several bank transfers including Federal Reserve, more accounting, and finally a deposit to the supplier's account. This process may involve anywhere from three or four weeks' delay, in the case of a simple local charge account, to as much as two or three months if national accounts are involved. In contrast, as the example of Jack Smith illustrates, transfers of value through

1. Speech by Martin Greenberger at the American Bankers' Assocation Annual Meeting, San Francisco, 1965.

SAVE will take place at exactly the same time as the transaction.

The general objectives of SAVE are clear. Great economic advantages to nearly all segments of business, finance, and consumers will result from providing rapid and paperless settlements among the elements in a community that are involved in buying and selling and debtor-creditor relationships.

SAVE will dramatically decrease float. It will eliminate the need for most currency and keep the value represented by the currency invested. It will tend to increase the number of deposits and loans, because traditional accounts receivable will appear instead as additional money in the suppliers' accounts and accounts payable may well become short-term loans.

For banks or other organizations providing the overdraft lending pool funds, SAVE will provide a major new "lower end" consumer and organizational loan or short-term credit business potential. By having all banks in a community become subscribers to SAVE, there will no longer be any handling of foreign items or interbank clearings as such; there would be no float, no NSF's, no holds, and no stops. For merchants or retailers, the added costs of being in the credit business will be eliminated. (See footnote 2 below for proof that retailers lose money on credit business.)

The vast expenses involved in most organizations in accounts receivable, billing, collections, payables, payroll, check writing, sorting, mailing, and handling will be greatly reduced. With tighter control over purchase authorization and cash withdrawals, the SAVE substitute for check cashing, bad debts, and bad check losses, together with collection costs, will be substantially reduced.

Value running into many millions of dollars annually will be added to the total national economy. According to Green-

2. Two cost of credit studies made by Touche, Ross, Bailey & Smart in 1963 and 1968 for the National Retail Merchants' Association. Available from NRMA, New York City.

berger, when the system operates on a truly nationwide basis, it should have a positive effect on business cycles. A tendency toward smoothing should occur, because the system can provide as little or as much delay as is desired between the actual producing of goods and services and the exchange of value for them. This point has not been mentioned, but SAVE could introduce programmed delays in the exchange between accounts, either locally or among metropolitan area centers. This action would be, in effect, programmed or controlled float.

SAVE will encompass virtually all bill paying activity and eliminate for Jack Smith the time consuming job of collecting, sorting, checking, and adding up his monthly bills, matching them against his ability to pay, writing and mailing checks, and keeping records of the details of his personal or family budget. A budget management service will be provided by SAVE, which will be described later in this chapter.

A reduction in the cost of "credit" for the consumer should also result from SAVE. The word "credit" is in quotes here, because actually the bulk of the consumer transactions will be essentially cash transactions. If interest free "credit" is injected for 30 to 45 days, this should be regarded as a cash situation. Therefore, the reduction will really be in the cost of moving goods and services rather in the cost of "credit."

One additional advantage for the consumer will be a thinner wallet and thus less wear on pockets or pocketbooks. There will be only one card in Jack Smith's wallet and practically no cash. He will be able to obtain cash nearly anywhere when he needs it and will never cash a check. Pickpockets will go out of business.

continuation of save example

Suppose Mrs. Smith goes on a shopping trip the day after Jack bought the vacuum cleaner. At the grocery store she presents her SAVE card at the checkout counter. The store follows the same procedure Jack saw at Universal Retail, except that it would be speeded up because of the line of people waiting behind Mrs. Smith. If she is well-known in the store, the checkout clerk may override the identity step, enter the total amount, insert the card, and receive an immediate "Purchase authorized" indication plus printed slip. Common practice will not require Mrs. Smith's signature. SAVE matches her identity number from the card with the Smith family account by looking in an index. Both Jack's and his wife's cards will probably have their respective Social Security numbers encoded.

Mrs. Smith knows she is going next door to the small doughnut counter shop that requires cash and she also needs some change for the parking meter and gum machine for Johnny. So she asks the grocery clerk for $10 cash. The transaction is handled exactly the same way, except that the clerk punches the "CASH WITHDRAWAL" key, and an immediate exchange of value is made of $10.00 between the grocery's account and the Smith family account. The grocery has no concern over this transaction, because it is guaranteed by SAVE that $10.00 has been added to the store account. As long as the cash is available in the drawer at the terminal, Mrs. Smith will get what she needs. This illustrates the fourth basic SAVE service, cash withdrawal. This service might be looked upon as a means of keeping a small but essential part of the economy operating.

By the time Mrs. Smith gets home, she may have generated seven or eight SAVE transactions of the purchase authorization type, including grocery store, bakery, gas station, department store, and children's clothing store. She also might stop at the drive-in bank to make a deposit or withdrawal or a loan payment. This occurrence, however, is not too likely in the SAVE world of the future, because such transactions will be handled in a different manner or at a different place.

Each community with a SAVE center will have a downtown SAVE office and suburban or exurban offices conveniently located either separately or as part of the major bank subscribers' offices. Let us say that the Smiths live in a suburb of the city of St. Francisburg and have their account at the First National Bank there. Once a year or perhaps oftener they will visit the suburban branch of First National. The bank will be their interface with SAVE. In fact, they may not even know SAVE exists. As far as the Smiths are concerned, they do business with, receive overdrafts from, receive periodic statements from, pay interest to, and receive family budgeting advice from First National.

Figure 4-1   SAVE functional diagram.

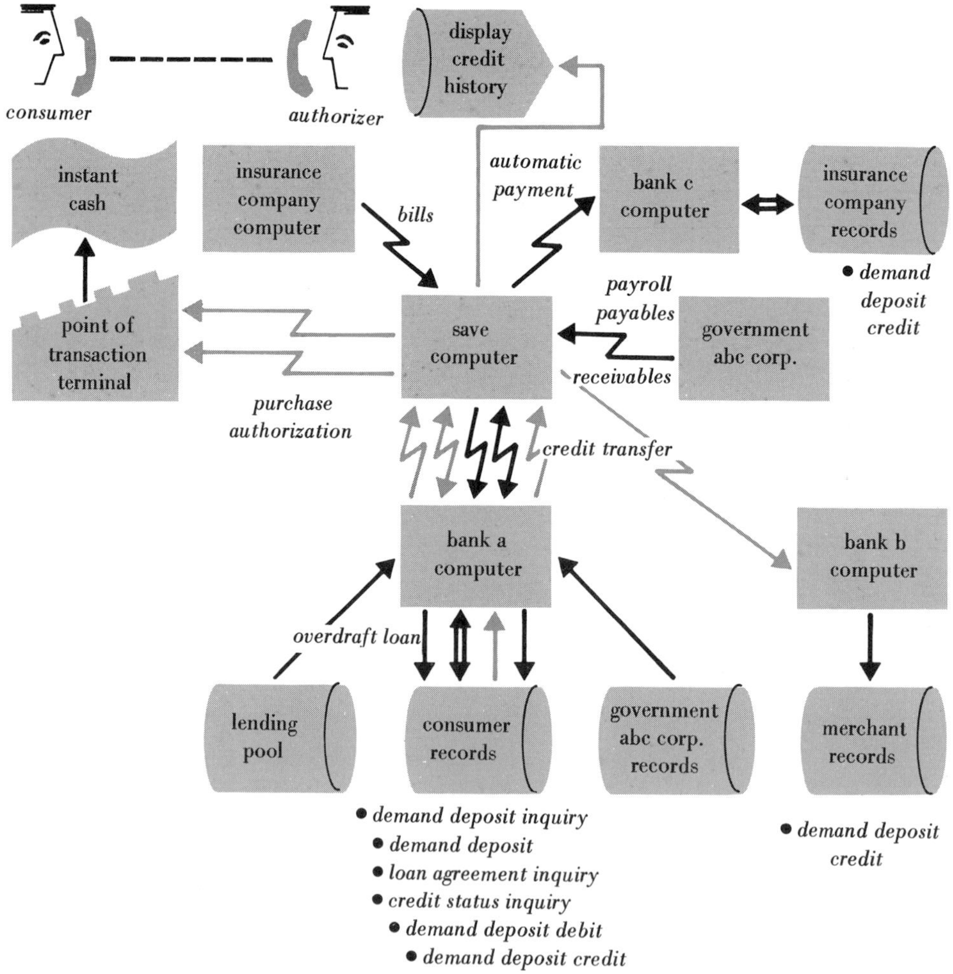

When the Smiths arrived in St. Francisburg, they had achieved a fair credit and banking record in their former community. So when they opened an account at First National, a good bank and credit record was received from the SAVE center in the other city. Jack sat down with his account executive at the bank during the first week in town, and a line of overdraft credit of $1000 was set for the family. Jack also decided with Mrs. Smith to subscribe to a family budgeting service.

They purchased a house with a mortgage at a local savings and loan association, which gave them a better deal than First National. The payments for the first year were $123.71 per month including taxes. Jack filled out a short form at the savings and loan bank, which authorized First National (SAVE) to transfer $123.71 from his account to the S & L account every month until further notice. These transfers took place on the dot on the 23rd of each month until a tax increase in the middle of the second year pushed the payments to $125.62. Jack signed a small form sent to him by the savings and loan association to authorize the increase in the transfer, again until further notice. This example illustrates the fifth type of SAVE service, automatic bill payment for a fixed amount. Other payments in this category were on the refrigerator and color TV, which the Smiths financed through dealers.

The other SAVE services are listed in Table 4-1 and are shown in the functional diagram of Figure 4-1.

impact on organizations

Up to now the impact on the individual citizen has been presented. SAVE will have a substantial impact on virtually every organization in the country. Perhaps those most affected will be banks and retailers.

In general, from the retailer's point of view, the major advantage of SAVE will be the opportunity to get out of the credit and accounts receivable business altogether. At the same time, a potential will exist for obtaining much more detailed information about cash customers as well as credit customers. The headaches of being in the credit business will disappear, while the main benefit, namely customer contact and relationship, will be retained and strengthened.

Several factors linking bankers and retailers have created the pressure for SAVE. Since World War II, banks have been and are under continuing pressure from competing institutions and their own customers to provide a variety of new customer services, including a variety of retail services, for both businesses and individuals. An automatic financial clearing process such as SAVE can be viewed in part as an extension of this trend. Moreover, it has so many ramifications in other parts of a bank's business that it is viewed not merely as a new service and a new source of profit but as dramatically supporting the traditional loan and deposit relationships between the bank and its retail and other business customers.

The technological feasibility for SAVE exists as a result of major information utility advances. The technology involved in SAVE, combining computers, communications, and special terminal devices, is certainly no more formidable than that of the general purpose information utility described in Chapter 3.

In addition, the emergence of new professional groups in banks, communications companies, computer manufacturers, and others is pushing their organizations in this new direction. As business relationships change, as new techniques come to the fore, these professionals are pressuring their own managements to exploit the opportunities arising from the technological fallout taking place now almost daily. Furthermore, strong entrepreneurial interests see a golden opportunity in making the SAVE concept profitable.

Another pressure for SAVE is the explosive growth in personal and installment credit. The growth, universal acceptance, and use of credit by individuals is illustrated most dramatically by the accelerating trends of both installment and noninstallment credit since 1950. This increase has begun to have a profound effect on the growth of problems retailers face in handling credit. The costs, the number of accounts, the credit cards, the statements mailed, the credit checks, etc., are multiplying in a seemingly profligate and unnecessarily burdensome way. The NRMA's cost of credit studies made in 1963 and 1968 show retailers are losing money by being in the credit business.

However, there will be important questions to be answered that are of concern to the retailer and to his customers:

1. What will the costs of SAVE be to the retailer? Will SAVE cost less than the present cost of credit, especially if the present income from retail revolving and installment accounts is assumed to be taken away from the retailer?

2. Will SAVE cause an overall increase or decrease in total sales for the retailer?

3. Will the retailer be able to retain or to improve the image he has today with his charge account customers? Will SAVE cause a loss of contact and public relations value between the store and its best customers?

4. Will it be possible to reach customers with advertising and promotional material as has been the case in the past?

5. What will replace the accounts receivable file in providing information for sales analysis and forecasting?

6. Will there be any problem in security if a retailer's customer files are, in effect, the property of SAVE?

7. Who becomes responsible for collections and bad debt losses? How will the retailer's customer react if he is refused SAVE credit on the sales floor?

In addition to these considerations, many large retailers may wish to participate financially in the operation, ownership, and profit of SAVE. If banks or others become the prime movers in developing SAVE, what role can be taken by the retailer and, in many cases, the credit bureau that he owns or controls? Evaluations of retailer reactions indicate that most of these questions for the retailer will be answered in the affirmative, if SAVE is properly implemented.

The impact on other commercial organizations will be

substantial in the areas of payroll transfers, bill payment transfers, and budgeting and cash management.

And who will participate in SAVE transactions? Nearly every individual and all organizations in one way or another. The mechanics of how every organization in the country would be provided the SAVE services remains somewhat indeterminate. One possible physical arrangement would be a series of SAVE centers in metropolitan areas across the country, all interlinked by data communications.

Within a community the SAVE utility may resemble Figure 4-2. The SAVE terminals in each organization will vary depending on the subscriber's peculiarities. For example, the retailer will have a point of sale device connected on line to his own OLRT system or else to a retail IU in the community. That same device will serve to handle SAVE

Figure 4-2   System for Automatic Value Exchange—
SAVE. All locations in a metropolitan area.

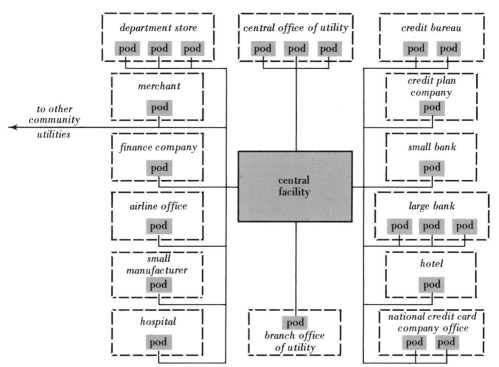

transactions, since it must already possess all of the necessary SAVE characteristics as a result of the retailer's own requirements. Bank terminals will also be patterned after the banker's own OLRT systems needed for other than SAVE purposes.

How does SAVE stand today? Payment Systems, Inc., is the leading commercial contender to provide SAVE services. Banks, the Federal Reserve, and several other organizations are also potential suppliers. One thing is certain: SAVE will be the most highly regulated IU of all.

5 *ticketing service (trs)*

An on-line ticketing service was proposed in 1962.[1] In 1968 the first, and perhaps the only, ticketing service information utility went into operation.

Of all the IU's described so far, the ticketing service is the one tending most toward a single supplier situation. The commodity being sold is really tickets, as well as information about tickets, to any reserved seat performance of any kind throughout the world. The performances include legitimate theatre, motion picture theatres, sporting events, musical events, educational institution reserved seat events, and, yes, even political conventions and meetings.

The following detailed description is based primarily upon the existing IU, Ticket Reservation Services, whose headquarters and data center is in New York City. TRS serves subscribers in most major cities in the United States and Canada. It offers most of the types of tickets mentioned above.

concept

The ticketing service IU concept is relatively simple at first glance. Producers of events or owners of reserved seats for events, place their inventory of seats, individually designated, in the IU central storage. These seats can be stored for as much as a year in advance of the event but usually will be placed in on-line storage whenever ticket sales generally begin in any quantity.

Subscribers to the service are ticket sellers. They may be seat owners or event producers in some cases, but usually

1. Richard E. Sprague, *Electronic Business Systems* (New York: The Ronald Press Company, 1962).

they are agents. An agent selling theatre tickets or sporting event tickets may be a sporting goods store, a department store, a credit card organization, a travel agent, a theatre agent, or any one of a thousand other types. In fact, the ticket service IU concept not only makes it possible for a far greater number of organizations or people to become agents, but the IU finds it advantageous to promote the idea of really mass distribution.

The seat owners are delighted to be able to have many more agents anywhere in the country sell their tickets with complete assurance of accuracy and with inventory status known at all times up to the latest second. The public is also delighted because they can be assured on the spot of possessing a ticket for the seat they want, or the closest available alternative, no matter where the event is located or where the purchase is made. There is absolute assurance that all seats unsold are made available for perusal every time anyone anywhere makes a purchase. Furthermore, the purchaser has his ticket in hand right away, or if he uses his telephone and buys on credit, he is assured that the exact seats he purchased will be held for him at the box office. A theatre-goer living in San Francisco and flying to New York for a vacation with his family, can purchase, in San Francisco, tickets to the play he wants to see on Broadway. There is no more waiting for confirmation, only to be denied after a week or two. Nor is any influence necessary with friends in New York. And there are no wasted phone calls trying to find something that is not sold out.

Another by-product of the ticketing service is the reduction of "ice," the term for semilegitimate markup of prices by owners, agents, or others. The control over "ice" comes primarily because there are *no* preprinted tickets, which someone can hoard and then sell at the last minute. All tickets are printed only at the time and place of a sale. Furthermore, refunding or exchanging of tickets can be controlled much more efficiently because of the elimination of the allocation system.

The owner of the seats, in some cases, may reserve the

right to print a batch of tickets at the box office for the event itself. This printing would be done to shorten the waiting lines for last hour box office purchases. Reserved seats at a baseball game are a good example of this situation, where many more purchases are made at the time of the event than, for example, at a Broadway play.

At any rate, the key part of the concept is, of course, the on-line connection from the agent's terminal to the central inventory of seats. This factor has for many years been the key to success of airline reservation systems. In the ticketing service, however, one more feature has been added: the on-line printing of the ticket as the seat is removed from inventory.

operation

From the subscriber point of view, the operation of the service seems straightforward, again at first glance. The customer comes in or phones in and asks about a performance of an event. The agent enters the date and event description by keyboard or other means on his terminal. If the customer has specified a particular seat or type of seat, the service tells the agent whether it is available or not. If it is, the service indicates a seat number or location, and the agent quotes this information along with the price to the customer. If the customer says, "I'll take it," the agent proceeds to inform the IU that he is selling the seat whereupon the IU removes it from inventory and prints out a ticket on the agent's terminal.

Sounds simple, but consider what may happen. Taking a popular Broadway play as an example, the assumption can be made that it is sold out for some period ahead. But is it? "Sold out" usually means there are some single seats left, or some seats in the upper balcony, or behind a post. So the customer who wanders in off the street by himself, fifteen minutes before the performance, and wants to pick up a canceled or returned ticket must still be accommodated.

Assume, however, that our customer follows the normal procedure and says, "I'm going to be in New York for two weeks next June. Do you have two seats on the aisle in the orchestra beginning June 12 for any of the next 13 days?" Now that is not a simple question for the service to answer. First of all, the customer asked for two seats together. He could have made it worse and asked for five. The IU must not only look for available seats but available pairs of seats, or triplets, or quadruplets, etc.

Second, the customer did not specify one date, so the IU must search through 13 dates. A transaction called "first available" is sometimes used to search for the first performance, beginning today, that has the specified number and location open.

Third, the customer wants orchestra seats and on the aisle. This specification means more searching. And each additional complexity in searching is usually coupled with additional storage requirements in the IU's memory.

Now suppose the answer is "not available," and the IU is programmed to display the best available alternate, or else the customer asks for it. The question is: What determines the best alternate? Are two seats way in the back, in a corner of the orchestra, better or worse than two seats midway back in the center of the first balcony? The agent obviously is forced into an interactive mode with the IU and an exploratory situation with the customer. By eliminating or narrowing down the possibilities with the customer, the agent can reduce the number of availability transactions with the IU.

The tricky part comes after the customer says, "I'll buy." Remember that hundreds of agents all over the United States are selling tickets at the same time; therefore, the inventory status of the play in question will be continuously changing. The two seats just agreed upon as being available might be "sold out from under" the customer before the agent can push the "Sell" button. This situation can easily happen if the customer has been exploring several alternatives and finally chooses one that had been queried several transactions back.

The solution to this problem is to have the IU "block,"

or hold temporarily out of active inventory, seats that are displayed to the agent as being available. Then as he presses the "Sell" button, they are removed completely. But what if the customer does not want the seats, or what if the agent "blocks" several pairs of seats and sells only one pair? In this case, the IU measures a specified elapsed time of "blocking" and then automatically puts them back into inventory again. If the agent knows what this specified time is, he can "reblock" them by making another availability call.

special problems

Other complications can arise, depending on the type of event and the customer's desires. Generally the IU "maps" the seats in its memory according to the way they are usually requested. For example, at baseball games it is customary to specify first base side or third base side, behind home plate, between the bases, boxes or reserved seats, tier above the field, etc.

Dressing the House   One oddity of a legitimate theatre is called "dressing the house." Through the years, experience has shown that actors are influenced by the grouping of the audience when the house is sparsely filled. Their reaction to seeing a small knot of people all sitting down front in the center of the orchestra is very poor. Their reaction to the same number of people distributed throughout the orchestra with empty seats between is better. So the IU must be programmed to perform this distribution automatically. This distribution of seats, of course, must be done as they are sold, because they can not be retracted as the performance date draws near.

Box Office Terminals   A special problem is created by large block sales to groups. These sales are handled through special terminals at the box office. In fact, box office terminals are provided with many special capabilities. They are equipped to handle canceled or returned tickets. They can, as mentioned earlier, cause printouts of large numbers of tickets just before performance time. They are equipped with special querying features that can give an overview of the status of inventory, and they have certain audit and control features, all of which the agents' terminals do not have.

marketing and competition

As mentioned earlier, the ticket service IU has a tendency to become noncompetitive. This is true because there is just one inventory of seats for any given event and only one IU can handle it. Since most reserved seat events occur in large metropolitan areas and since there are only a few areas for certain types of events, such as legitimate theatre, one IU obtaining rights to inventories of seats in a majority of these few areas will tend to obtain all of them.

Once agents anywhere in the United States install a terminal connected to one IU selling most events in the major cities, a certain reluctance begins to develop on the part of both agents and seat owners to install a second terminal or to place their inventory in the hands of a second competitive IU. Moreover, there is a bandwagon effect upon a seat owner who does not yet have his inventory placed with an IU. His competitive position, especially for sales outside his own area, is sharply reduced. A sharp ticket service entrepreneur can take full advantage of these "monopolistic" tendencies and eventually eliminate nearly all competition.

equipment

The central facility for the ticket service IU contains more or less conventional equipment. Special memory and software problems exist, however, because of the nature of ticket requests and seating plans described earlier.

The ticketing terminals have some unusual characteristics. The requirement for printing multicolored, hard copy, stiff paper, controllable, noncopyable tickets at remote terminals is primary. Query formats and the need for interaction, as described in the theatre ticket example, also produce some special features. The early terminals were keyboard oriented with layouts somewhat like airline, car rental, and hotel reservation terminals. Photographs of the agent terminals and box office terminals that were introduced by Ticket Reservation Services in 1968 are shown in Figure 5-1.

As the cost of CRT terminals lowers and as interactive techniques develop, in which the agents use a combination of CRT displays and point to items on the screen, the CRT with light pen will become quite useful in ticket services.[2]

2. This same conclusion can be reached about almost any IU where a great deal of interaction is required.

Figure 5-1   Ticket service terminal. (Courtesy Ticket Reservation Systems, Incorporated)

The pointing technique will replace button pushing, and the IU service will relieve the agent from much of his responsibility for pressing the correct keys. The box office terminals will probably be the first ones to be converted to CRT types since their requirements are more complex and there are fewer of them.

status

In late 1968, there were two main competitors for the ticket service market, Ticket Reservation Systems, Inc., of New York City, and Teleticketing Corporation, of Los Angeles, a subsidiary of Computer Sciences Corporation. As might be anticipated from their respective locations, TRS was strong in the Eastern markets, especially New York, while Teleticketing had achieved some market penetration on the West Coast. As 1969 began, TRS seemed to be the likely winner, if the monopolistic theory, described earlier, were to hold.

6

personal data services (pds)

The IU with perhaps the greatest long-range impact on individuals is that supplying personal data services.[1] Its impact on organizations will be felt indirectly through the change in abilities and actions of the individuals who manage them. Over a longer period of time there will also be an effect on the design of the management information systems of organizations.

Stated simply, the personal data services information utility will provide individuals with their own personal information services. It will be flexible enough to permit the individual, whether he or she is an executive, a student, or a housewife, to evolve his or her own services. It will, in the case of the executive, allow the evolution from his own personal services through larger and larger organizational units to compatibility with the total management information system of his organization.

concept

The concept of personal data services (PDS) is composed of several new and fundamental ideas about the use of computers, information systems, and information storage and retrieval techniques. It has grown out of a number of years of research on the largest unsolved problem in management information systems. The problem, simply stated, is: "What information does management *really* need to make decisions and to manage, and how do managers use it?"

Some observers have said this is an unsolvable problem

1. Personal data services (PDS) will be used in this book as a generic term for a concept and a type of IU service. The Recallit service of Ultronics (no longer available) had some of the characteristics of PDS.

and that management information systems designers will never discover what managers require.[2] Managers on their own will probably never discover what they need either. If the problem is insoluble, it is because it is fantastically complex. It sounds simple enough when posed as a single question, but that one question leads to a multitude of others, such as:

What is management and what is a manager?

What is information?

What is a decision?

What kinds of decisions do managers make and how?

Do managers perform their daily functions by making decisions, and what else do they do that requires information?

What impact on information systems do managers have?

What are the organizational relationships that affect managers' decisions and therefore the information required?

Does the information received by management affect the organizational relationships?

The fundamental question that comes up more and more is: "Why would a manager want to communicate directly with a system?" rather than "What information does he need?" This fundamental question could be put in the following form: "If a manager *could* communicate directly with a management information system, what information would he use in making decisions, or, more broadly speaking, what information would he use in just plain doing his job from day to day?"

Analysis of what a manager really does all day long (and at night too) in executing his responsibility reveals that very little of what he does is decision making in its traditional form. Yet, most managers really do need vast quantities of information to do what they do. They need it at their fingertips and in real time. The point about today's managers is that they do not have vast quantities of information at their

2. Robert Anthony, Conference on Management Information Systems (Cambridge, Mass.: The MIT Press, 1967).

fingertips, and they *do not* have whatever information they do have in real time.

It seems to take forever to obtain even the simplest information from the files, from a secretary or an assistant, or out of the manager's own memory. The manager of today is faced with a far more complex world with many more facets to any given decision and with a need for far more information and a greater complexity in the information than his grandfather. Yet, in spite of all the wonderful new techniques and tools produced so far by the information revolution, the manager is still using the same tools his grandfather used. These tools are the desk, the desk drawer, pencils, paper, files, telephone, calendar, address book, note pads, things to do listed on a small piece of paper, his own bad memory, and a secretary who is replaced every so often. Occasionally, one may also find on or near a manager's desk, a few tools not available to his grandfather. These may include a dictating machine, an automatic card dialing telephone with speaker phone, key sort card files, electric typewriters, etc. In technically oriented organizations, one may also find slide rules, desk calculators, adding machines, blackboards, flip charts, and drafting equipment. Certainly, he may have a few new tools. But are they really part of the information revolution? No!

And lest one jump to the conclusion that the people working for or around the manager are using new tools, and therefore will be able to help him in the near future, let it be said right away that they too are using the tools of their grandfathers.

The information utilities discussed earlier that were aimed at engineers, students, or doctors *have* begun to bring the impact of the new technology to individuals' minds. Several engineers out in the laboratory where the manager works are doing something new and strange. Maybe even some of the typists or secretaries around the place are. But this is a different world to the manager and to him has no obvious impact. His management information systems designers have not helped him personally. Even the fellow who had that terminal placed on his desk for a while soon threw it out.

To the average businessman, the fact that engineers, students, professors, a few doctors, and fewer secretaries are directly interacting with computers is either unknown or unrelated to his own everyday world. He finds it extremely difficult to imagine that a television set on his desk connected to a distant computer is anything but an expensive toy. Yet, the new generation of tools already being used by engineers and students does have a chance of releasing the manager from his dilemma. His only salvation in the space age world, in which more and more complex information is required to perform a manager's function, may very well be the use of personal data services.

Most of the statements just made also apply to the housewife and the ordinary citizen.

the personal information concept

The personal data service concept begins with a basic postulation, which is in the process of being scientifically proved and is intuitively reasonable. It is that, of all the information a manager or a housewife would or could use to perform his or her function in a more efficient, less frustrating, better way, a large portion of it is *personal* in nature. Conversely, the postulation states that very little of a manager's total information needs can or will ever come out of or be derived from a management information system in the traditional sense.

This part of the postulation tends to support or perhaps explain Anthony's statement that systems designers will never discover management's true information requirements. The "system" which Anthony is thinking about in this context is the traditional organizational management information system, which takes the dynamic functional flow of information and data through and into and out of the organization, and structures it in a systematic way.

The spectrum of a manager's information needs certainly

does include some of this kind of information, but the PDS theory is that the percentage is very small. The sources of information making up the bulk of his requirements lie outside his own organization's total management information system, even if one exists. Today, these sources are personal and nonmechanized in nature. They include the manager's own brain and memory, his secretary's brain and memory, his personal files, both in his desk and in his sections of the filing cabinets, the files of his own small organizational element, his Rolodex file, his calendar, his address book, his "things to do" list, etc.

In the case of the housewife, they include her memo pad by the phone, the little blue phone number book, the shopping list in her head or on scraps of paper, the check list of bills paid and unpaid, etc.

the partnership concept

The second important postulation of PDS theory is that a partnership can and should be formed between a human being and a computer or information system or service. This partnership will produce a synergistic effort, such that the resulting use of information will far exceed the sum of the individual capabilities of the man and the service.

To examine this postulation it is necessary to go back to some fundamental psychological ideas concerning information and thinking. It is impossible to separate the information requirements of the person from his requirements for other forms of assistance. Raw data, or information resulting from data, supplied to an individual without any relation to the current mental processes he will involve in using the information for decision making or just in carrying out his job will be largely superfluous.

The mental processes associated with information include reasoning, postulating, judgment, analysis, logical deduction, planning or forecasting, computing, interpolation, interpretation, remembering, and many others. Human beings perform some of these processes with more success than others. Moreover, the variations from one person to another in their abilities, for example, to remember and to reason logically are very great.

Information systems, on the other hand, far exceed the capability of humans in some of these functions. Remembering, in particular, can be done with greater accuracy and facility by a properly designed information storage and retrieval system than it can be by a human being. Computing, plus a certain amount of interpolation, interpretation, analysis, and logical deduction, can also be accomplished with greater efficacy by a computer system. The game playing capabilities of the more sophisticated computer programs, which can beat the average chess or checkers or bridge player most of the time, give an indication of some of this power.

An interactive partnership, combining the greatest capabilities of both men and a computer-information service, will produce a result greater than the sum of the two. The major contributions of the service to the partnership are memory and guidance. The relatively poor memory of the individual will, in effect, be extended in an unlimited fashion. Furthermore, this memory extension will not only apply to data and information (or facts) but to thought and reasoning processes. In other words, the computer service will interact with the man in such a manner as to help him remember how to accomplish the other mental processes mentioned earlier. In this new sense, the computer service does not do the reasoning or the logical deduction or the planning. Rather, it remembers what the user has told it to memorize about these processes, and it recalls these processes for the user upon the execution of an interactive instruction.

the guidance concept

The third idea of PDS is the guidance concept. This basic idea stems from several independent sources. First, in the field of education, programmed teaching and learning, further developed in the late 1960's into computer aided education, have contributed to the step-by-step instructional process. Second, engineering and scientific time sharing services have contributed an interactive capability in which the human being evolves an ever growing set of problem solving tools that are remembered and "played back" upon request by the time-shared computer service. Third, the information retrieval field, developing largely in library and technical reference service groups, has provided some new schemes, using interactive techniques, for aiding an individual in storing, indexing, and retrieving information. Fourth, various military and government sponsored projects have produced some generalized data management languages that will enable a service to guide the user through a set of steps simple to understand, yet extremely complex from a computer programming point of view.

The combination of these ideas results in a human-to-service and service-to-human communication technique, which cannot properly be called a *language* in the information systems or programming sense. The "language" being used is really a visual-pictorial one, although textual information can be communicated back and forth in the human's native tongue.

The service always leads the user through a series of displayed choices or selections.[3] At each step of the process, the human user can pick one of several possible things from the display. He may choose one of several pieces of information, or he may choose one of several action steps to be taken next. The choices are always simple and easily understood. The service supplies these choices, however, at the discretion and instruction of the human.

This element is somewhat like a reminder pad or tape recording. The individual tells the service what facts he wishes to remember and how they are related. He also tells the service how to remind him to ask for these facts to be played back. The result is a truly cybernetic system in which it is difficult to tell whether the human is guiding the service or the service is guiding the human.

---

3. The word "display" is used here in a very general sense. A cathode ray tube (CRT) display is not necessarily implied.

Use of a series of interactive guided choices of displays may produce a rote procedure that requires no more thought than dialing an often used telephone number. These rote steps may in some cases permit the user to condense the number of displayed steps by changing the action selections.

organizational relationships

The fourth postulation of the PDS concept is that personal data files for individuals in the same organizational unit will overlap and can be combined. However, each member of the unit will retain his or her personal files and individual ways of using the service. Organizational relationships will be affected by PDS, and vice versa.

A minimum organizational unit that might be proposed and used to test PDS theory includes a manager and his secretary. Their combined use of PDS will be more tightly coupled than other units. The manager may desire that his secretary be able to substitute for him in communicating directly with his own personal files. He himself may never wish to enter new data into the files but rather will always have his touch typing secretary enter it for him. The secretary may communicate with PDS in a somewhat different manner than her boss. For example, she may use PDS for typing assistance, analogous to Datatext,[4] or she may make more extensive use of an index service to locate things in manual files, which will still exist.

Manager and secretary may each have their own personal files but share such things as a business name, address and phone number file. At home, husband, wife, and children may begin to share files.

As the organizational unit grows in size, more complex relationships will be found in the PDS usage by the individual members and the entire unit as a whole. Administrative or office managers will make different use of PDS than will line personnel working for the same manager. File clerks, staff assistants, secretaries, typists, and other clericals will all use PDS in differing ways.

4. Datatext is an on-line typing-editing service supplied by IBM.

When most members of an organizational unit, like a geographically isolated office or a department, have begun to use PDS, an office or departmental data base or set of files will begin to develop. Eventually, a collection of personal data bases will evolve into a departmental data base. Several of these can evolve into a divisional or company management information system. The latter possibility is likely only if the organization has not already undertaken a planned program to design a management information system in the more traditional sense.

self-design and programming

One of the problems associated with the question, "What information does a manager really need?" is the task of programming a system to give the manager what he requires. This task has been regarded by many as being almost as difficult as discovering what he needs. With the current shortages of programmers, the question is: "Who would do the programming for the management information systems of the future, even if we *could* determine management's true requirements for information?"

PDS will supply the answer to this problem by permitting the manager, or any other user, in effect, to do his own programming and systems design. Actually, there will be two levels of programming involved in PDS. The highest level will be a superdata management language, evolving from the military-government developments. The superlanguage will take care of all bookkeeping tasks connected with information storage allocations and will also provide automatic retrieval of interlinked information or data elements. The chaining technique[5] built into the superlanguage will allow a piece of information to be found by means of a number of different descriptors.[6] The superlanguage will

5. One leading example of chaining can be found in the Microplex language developed by General Electric Company's Deacon Project.
6. A *descriptor*, in information retrieval technology, is one identifying piece of data. Several descriptors combined will specifically identify a file or item of information.

also allow second level programming to be accomplished by a user interacting directly with his own set of files and "programs."

The second level language is the interactive one that the human user employs. He will not think of it as a language, nor will he think of his actions as "programming."[7] The only reason to label what happens as "programming" is that the user is changing several different things that happen to the data he is storing, retrieving, and displaying. He is changing the descriptors and the chains interrelating various data. He is changing the formats of display, and, more significantly, he is changing the guidance instructions and selections displayed to him by the service.

The service, controlled by the superlanguage, must provide the user with simple, easily understood guidance in the procedure of changing these various things. This guidance, in effect, is computer-directed programming instruction without appearing to be.

The overall effect of a group of individuals, such as a departmental manager, line personnel, staff personnel, secretaries, file clerks and other clericals, administrative and office managers, and research assistants all doing their own "programming" to one extent or another, is one that will require some research and testing. However, PDS theory states that in the long run there should be a net saving in programming workloads for management information systems.

personal involvement

PDS will, by its very nature, *involve* the manager, or the executive, or the secretary in a brand-new way. The personal involvement in the evolution of a data base, in the information content, and in the manner in which it is utilized should bring about a new level and type of interest. As soon as one manager begins to use the new PDS tools, all managers at his

7. Henceforth, the word "programming" in quotation marks will refer to this second level type of activity.

level or above and below will want to have access to PDS as well. Cutting horizontally across an organization, a desire for the PDS tools will affect secretaries, accountants, researchers, and clericals alike.

At the same time, one of the basic problems in traditional management information systems will be avoided or greatly reduced. This problem concerns a higher level manager gaining access to information before a lower level manager can, or vice versa. When the design concept for an MIS involves *only* one impersonal management information data base, conflicts are bound to develop among managers and other people at various levels. The result is exaggeration of organizational, political, and psychological problems. To put it another way, a major concern of systems designers has been to *prevent everyone* in the organization from gaining direct on line–real time access to all information in the data base. Complex, expensive (to program) sets of file security techniques have been devised to solve this problem.

The PDS concept, on the other hand, provides an automatic file security system. Since each personal data base is evolved by the individual in a unique personal way, it will be extremely difficult for another individual to make head or tail of the information in it. Of course, the superlanguage must protect each data base from being changed except by the individual or someone he designates.

The jealousies inherent in direct access to a single organizational MIS should disappear or be greatly reduced by PDS. Every user will have direct access to his own data base. Access to a departmental or total organizational data base will follow the lines of personal security that the organizational element desires. The roadblocks created by human beings to the progress of MIS will be turned into creative elements by the PDS concept.

the poor, tired executive

The men near or at the top of our largest organizations, whether these be corporations, government agencies or universities, are all plagued by the problems of too much to manage, too much to remember, too many decisions to make, and not enough time. Time is their most valuable commodity. Whatever is done to help the harassed executive must take a minimum amount of his time.

A tool that is too complex to learn or that takes too much time to use will never become popular. It is not that the average executive does not possess the intelligence to understand a new tool. It is just that he does not have enough time. He cannot afford as much as a week or two per year to go to school. He must, as the expression goes, keep eight or ten balls in the air for about 100 hours a week. That leaves just enough time to eat, sleep, and shave. It is this immense pressure that has kept most information systems tools from becoming popular among executives. The tools require too much time to permit the executive to learn how to save time by using them.

The executive has another characteristic that causes him no end of concern. In the new world where it is essential to remember more and more, the average older executive cannot remember anything. Furthermore, his secretary has trouble helping him to remember things and so do his staff members. Sometimes a new secretary cannot find anything in the files and neither can the executive, who could not find his way through any files because he has never been near them. Faces are hard enough to remember, but the executive has trouble with names too. Names of people important to him, to his organization, and to his daily life are difficult. Moreover, the affiliations of these people cannot be remembered. Of course, he has *never* memorized addresses or telephone numbers but relies on his secretary or Rolodex file or little black book. Of late, he has been forgetting to put numbers in the book. This is only the beginning of the things the poor, tired, old executive should remember but cannot.

Some other personal habits will be of importance in the design of PDS tools for the executive. He is no key pusher. He cannot type, nor even hunt and peck very well. He dislikes pushing any complex set of buttons. He cannot remember codes and does not want to. He will not tolerate a noisy device in his office. If something new is introduced to him, he may remember it for a while, but another exposure at a later date finds no recollection of it in his mind.

Now, not every executive has all of these characteristics. Some may have photographic memories, and others may understand and be fascinated with codes. But, any successful PDS will have to cope with all kinds of executives. Perhaps the most common characteristic will be a fanatical resistance to being systematized. Human judgment, foresight, intuition, hunch, and the final word over *any* information system will be the order of the day. For this reason, the direct use of PDS by executives *must* be considered as a set of tools to be used as the executive sees fit and not as an extension of a management information system.

pds design

The design of PDS will be an ever changing one, as research and testing in "live" office environments produce new requirements. However, it will be necessary to begin testing with a certain minimum combination of equipment and software. The probable minimum testing environment will be a manager and his secretary. The reason for this setup is the necessity for initial data input and continuing need for entering relatively large amounts of information. The manager will not want to perform this function, and a secretarial touch typing capability is needed for speed and accuracy of data input.

So, the minimum equipment required will be a manager's terminal and a secretary's terminal, plus a computer or a time sharing service capable of driving two terminals and also capable of holding the minimum software package. CRT terminals are probably a desirable minimum for testing purposes, so data communications equipment will have to be of voice grade design or better. File equipment will probably have to be a combination of discs and drums.

The minimum initial software package will have to be a

*Figure 6-1   Artist's conception of a personal
data services terminal. (Courtesy Personal
Data Services Corporation)*

data management language of the "super" type described
earlier. As PDS research and testing progresses, a less expensive more tailored superlanguage will no doubt evolve.
Existing languages are much too complex and powerful,
since they were designed originally with different objectives.

Terminal design should be adapted to the individual
user's tastes and personal habits. As mentioned earlier, the
manager will probably feel most comfortable with a quiet,
voluminous display device with a minimum number of keys.
A light pen type of terminal is probably most desirable. Future developments may make a touch terminal, like the one
in Figure 6-1, the best choice. On the other hand, the secre-

tary will be happier with a typewriter keyboard and possibly will be able to adapt to a CRT display, although initially a typewriter platen may be necessary. In the beginning, at least one of the terminals should be equipped with an output printer. If it is part of the manager's terminal, it must be quiet and fast. The Motorola and SCM printers would be usable.

A teaching program should be included in the initial software, so that manager and secretary can learn to use their terminals and the service with little or no other instruction.

types of service and files

The entire PDS concept is aimed at allowing the user to define his own set of files, or personal data base, and to decide how he will use them. For this reason, it will be impossible in the early stages of PDS to predict what a comprehensive set of services will be. It is even more difficult to predict what kinds of information or data files will be set up. The housewife's files will differ substantially from the executive's files. This is, in fact, exactly the problem said to be unsolvable by Anthony.

Nevertheless, a manager or secretary who is just beginning will need some guidance and some hints as to what data files and services *can* be established. The teaching program should start a beginner off with a suggested complement of data files and services. In the following section is a suggested set of files drawn up from the personal desires and experience of a management consultant. It may or may not be similar to a typical set designed by a marketing or sales executive or manager.

data files

File 1: Names—Individuals   This file will be comparable to the name section of a personal diary. It will contain the names of all individuals of importance to the user. Each name will be associated with several other descriptors. The principal location for some of these items may be in the name file itself, or chain pointers can lead to each of the descriptors. Some possible items are: business address and phone number, home address and phone number, prime organization affiliation, title, short description of responsibility, secondary organization of importance to relationship to user (examples: professional societies, social groups, private clubs, etc.), coded indication of prime relationship (examples: customer, employee, friend, business associate, etc.), dates, places, and purposes of recent and near future contacts (see calendar file), index to correspondence files, chain pointers with coded indications of interindividual relationships of importance (example: Mr. X works for Mr. Y, who makes purchasing decisions.)

File 2: Names—Organizations This data file will contain names of all organizations of importance to the user. Other descriptors will be: principal address and phone number, type of business or function, subsidiary names, addresses and phone numbers, chain pointers to each important individual in the organization, coded indication of prime relationship of organization to user and his own organization, dates, places, and purposes of recent and near future contacts, index to correspondence and literature, etc., files, chain pointers with coded indications of interorganizational relationships of importance.

File 3: Calendar This file will correspond to a person's appointment calendar or "week at a glance" diary or both. It will contain data on past and future appointments probably for a period of three to six months in both directions. For each time period of each day, either the file itself or other files pointed to by chains will contain: place and type of appointment or activity, individuals and organizations involved, purpose of appointment or activity, chain pointers to dates and times of related appointments, index to memo or report files concerning appointment. In his own data files, along with the manager's own calendar, will be the calendars of those people surrounding him in the organization whose schedules he would normally have access to.

File 4: Current Activity File   This file will be comparable to a person's "things to do" list, or "work in progress" file, or reminder list. It can include: "hot" items for today, correspondence or memos requiring action, outstanding telephone calls, actions to be delegated to the secretary or to others, coded indicators of priorities, etc.

File 5: Correspondence, Etc., File Index   This file can be maintained separately or it can be contained within data files 1, 2, and 3. It will enable a brand-new secretary or a harassed executive to find anything in the manual files. New information retrieval indexing schemes will be used, although they must be nearly automatic and simple for the various users of this file, which is presumed to be common to an organizational unit.

An interlock is needed between the manual filing procedure and this index, so that absolute 1 to 1 correspondence by physical location is assured. Thus, locations of manual files that are "on loan" will be included.

File 6: Travel   This file will be kept by the executive or manager who travels a lot. It can include records of recent and future itineraries and can serve as a working file for the secretary who makes reservations and travel arrangements for her boss. It can include a list, by city, of favorite hotels and airline schedules, as well as restaurants, clubs, resorts, meeting places, etc. that are popular for client or customer entertainment.

services

Service 1:   Finds an item in the data files, given a set of descriptors. In this operation, the user will specify a complete enough set of descriptions to allow PDS to find the item

94

in one user operation. PDS may have to follow through many chain pointers to locate and display the item.

Service 2:   Guides the user to a record, beginning with a limited set of descriptors. In this operation, the user will interact with PDS in several steps to find the item. For example, the user may be trying to remember the name of a person who attended a meeting in his office several months ago. He cannot recall the exact date but knows it within a few weeks. PDS guides him through a series of steps, displaying sections of his calendar, until he finds the correct meeting, and then displays the details of the meeting. Conversely, he may remember the man's name but not the date and time of the meeting.

Service 3:   Adds an item to the data files with chain pointers. In this operation, the user adds or changes an item in the data files, and PDS guides him through a series of steps to make sure all of the desired interrelationships between the new item and other items are entered in the file by means of chain pointers. For example, a new name of an individual will be entered and pointers entered connecting him with his organization, a professional society, a specified meeting, a correspondence file index, etc.

Service 4:   Locates an item in correspondence files. This service would combine Service 2 and the manual file index File 5 to assist a manager or, more particularly, a secretary or file clerk in finding items in correspondence, report, literature, and other manual files.

The success of this service will depend on the File 5 indexing scheme and the interlock described earlier. Usually, trouble in finding an item in the files begins because neither the boss nor the secretary can remember enough things about it to tie down how it was filed. Commonly, the only way the item is found is to look for it in a chronological file of correspondence. Service 4 will supply the user with whatever the user *can* remember about the item of interest. Chain pointers and interactive user-PDS displays of alternative choices will move the user toward the proper manual file location.

Service 5:   Displays all items in a given category. This service will select all items having the same set of descriptors and display them if there are not too many. If there *are* too many, the service will tell the user how many items there are and give a choice of whether to display them or whether to add more descriptors, narrowing down the number of items.

Service 6:   Displays all relationships of an item. This service will show the user all of the relationships between an item and all other items.

Service 7:   Changes a display. This service will allow the user to alter the display format.

Service 8:   Changes a list. The user can change the list of items being displayed.

Service 9:   Changes an operation or service.

input tricks

It will be desirable to reduce to a minimum the amount of time needed by the manager for input of information and also to reduce to a minimum the number of keys to be pressed. As mentioned under the section on the harried executive, the manager's time is his most valuable commodity. Any trick that PDS can utilize to cut down time will enhance the use of the concept.

The interactive guidance technique, combined with the flexibility of a CRT display and a light pen, can be used in many tricky new ways. In the following sections, only a few of the possibilities are discussed. Research and testing should produce many more.

Keyboard Display: A keyboard, either alphabetic or numeric, can be displayed on the CRT. The user can point to numbers and letters on the screen as a substitute for punching keys. The display can be made to look like a typewriter keyboard or can be shown in alphabetic sequence in rows, or in a circular arrangement, or in several other formats. As the user "types" by pointing, the items can be made to appear on part of the screen just as it would on a typewriter platen.

List Displays: Data already in the files can be displayed in the form of a series of lists interacting with the user. This method will reduce the necessity of entering items to be displayed or to be searched for. Furthermore, lists of standard words or phrases can be displayed for selection where new combinations of these are to be assembled. Commonly used data elements, such as times, dates, purposes of meetings, characteristics of individuals or organizations, etc., will be displayed in groups or lists and selected by the user pointing to them.

Secretary Input: Whenever a manager or executive wants to add items to the data files, PDS can make it easy for his secretary to enter them from her own terminal under his direction. This can happen whether the manager is at his own terminal or telephoning from outside the office.

examples of pds usage

To see how PDS might be used, imagine a manager and secretary, each with a CRT terminal. Assume that the manager has a light pen and no keyboard and that the secretary has a typewriter keyboard plus platen. Assume that data files 1 through 6 already exist.

The manager arrives at his office in the morning and immediately turns on his terminal. A list of services and files is displayed, and he selects the current activity file, File 4, by pointing to it. The display then shows all current activities. If the details require more than one screenful of information, a summary of activities is displayed.

The manager remembers that because of a phone call he received at home last night, the hottest item has now become a contract negotiation. He has a new name to add as a result of the call, so he points to the contract negotiation item and tells his secretary to add the name in connection with the negotiation. A negotiating meeting is indicated for the day after tomorrow at 10:00 A.M. However, also as a result of the telephone call, the manager wants to schedule a preliminary meeting tomorrow afternoon. A new legal point is involved, and he needs the advice of the tax specialist in his corporation's legal firm.

He points to a list of files and selects a calendar. He picks out the one for tomorrow and takes a look at the time slots for the afternoon. He sees 3:00 and 4.00 P.M. open and then calls for the organization list. He points to the legal firm's name through a few list steps and then calls for the names of the lawyers of importance, since he is unable to remember the tax man's name.

He receives the name, phone number, and other data on the tax lawyer on his screen. By pointing to a special part of the screen and pressing an intercom button, he causes the display to appear on his secretary's screen, and he asks her to get the tax man on the phone. While waiting, he notes that on the screen there is something that rings a familiar bell. The tax man belongs to the Spring Valley Country Club. He goes back to the file list (returning to the list of files or services can always be done at any step) and selects the customer organization involved in the contract negotiation. He obtains a display showing John Snyder, who is the prime thorn in the negotiations so far, and confirms the point he remembered. John is a member of Spring Valley also. When his secretary gets the tax man on the phone, he sets up an appointment for tomorrow at 3:00 P.M. and makes a tentative golf date for himself and the tax man and Snyder on the coming weekend.

Meanwhile, he has switched the Snyder display to his

secretary's screen and, by means of an agreed-upon inter-com signal, asks her to get Snyder on his other line. Luckily, Snyder is in, and the manager is able to reconfirm the con-tract negotiation date as well as make the golf date while both the tax man and Snyder are on the phone.

Now, all of the above might have been easily accom-plished with the tools of his grandfather, except that his secretary has been working for him for only two weeks. She knows nothing about the law firm or the manual files or the customer's organization as yet. She would have taken ten or fifteen minutes to find out the tax man's name, look up the law firm and Snyder's phone numbers, etc.; whereas, the sequence just described, using the new tools, took place in less than five minutes and that included telephone time.

It has been more than a year since the manager played golf at Spring Valley, and he begins to wonder about another possibility. He calls for a list of Spring Valley members in his data files and is pleasantly surprised to find Calvin Brewer's name listed among five others he knows. Cal has just moved over as chief corporate loan officer at the First National Bank and will be a potential source of funds for financing the new contract. The fact that Cal belonged to Spring Valley had slipped his mind.

The PDS search for Spring Valley members (in Service 5) is not quite as simple as some of the other things the manager has done this morning. So he needs a little help in remembering how to go about it. He moves the name "Spring Valley Country Club" to a temporary storage place on his screen by pointing to a special store operation and points to the name. Then he returns to the list of services and selects Service 5. At this step he points to the word "Teach" and receives a display explaining how to execute Service 5.

The instructions say that a sentence will appear on the screen with blanks which must be filled in either by pointing ("typing") or by moving data from another part of the screen. The sentence reads: "Search for and display all _____ which are _____ the _____. The manager can move into any one of the blanks the item in temporary storage or any of the words displayed on the rest of the screen. He performs this operation by pointing at the word first, then at the operator labeled "Move," and then at the position of the blank. In this case, the manager points and moves the word "individuals" into the first blank, the words "members of" into the second blank, and the words "Spring Valley Country Club" from the temporary storage location into the third blank. Then he points to the operator labeled "Execute." It should be noted that he created this search sentence structure himself several months ago, and he can change it if he does not like it.

the housewife's files

PDS for the housewife will help her remember many things she cannot now remember. It may also do some computing and budgeting and storing and reporting for her if she runs the family finances. Combined with SAVE, PDS will make her life, and her husband's life, much more comfortable and change many of her modes of living. Take, for example, grocery shopping and stocking of supplies, which of course are related to cooking and meal planning. How many housewives today really plan or carry out any of these chores in an organized or efficient fashion? Some husbands would say their wives are not intelligent enough to do it. Believe it or not, the reasons they are not so systematic are just the same ones as those that plagued the tired executive. First, there is not enough time, and, second, there are only poor or nonexistent information tools.

The housewife's CRT terminal connected to the PDS information utility will give her a new set of tools to help her daily life. It probably should be located in the kitchen near the kitchen telephone, although for the budget management and bill paying service it perhaps should be in the den. If it were not for interference with the ball games, soap operas, or the kids' morning comics, the family TV set could be used.

The files Mrs. Housewife will create for herself will be an individual's file, a calendar file, and an organizational file, just like her executive husband's files at the office. Except for a "thing to do today" list, however, the similarity ends. She will have a grocery inventory file, a shopping list file, a meal planning file, and recipe files. She may have a cooking and meal preparation file as well. She will have a bill paying and budget file and certainly a children's activity file. The calendar will contain all important birthdays, anniversaries, holidays, club dates, scouting and children's school events dates, etc. Advance reminders of all these will be part of the calendar service function.

The grocery-meal-shopping service will keep her advised of the inventory status of all foods (frozen and non-frozen) and supplies and place automatically on the current shopping list those items that need replenishing. The service will measure food usage, forecast meal and food costs, and alert her if some item usage looks too high. It can also prepare food and grocery budgets for her along with meal planning. All of these services, mind you, are ones she created in the first place. They are her own budgetary rules and decisions on food usage.

Eventually, an inexpensive printer will print a copy of today's shopping list from the CRT display. Or if she prefers ordering by phone, by the year 1984, the service will, after dialing automatically, give the list over the phone to the supermarket grocer who has his own version of PDS, which receives it and triggers an automated grocery pickup and delivery system.

other users

The reader can visualize for himself how PDS might serve his own personal needs, whether he or she is a student, teacher, small businessman, lawyer, or engineer.

7 *lottery service*

lotteries

Toward the end of the 1960's, lotteries in the United States became a legitimate business and a popular method for raising funds in many states. Suddenly, in what seemed to be an overnight development, all fifty states and several possessions became potential customers for lottery systems. When these were added to the foreign markets, the possibility of supplying lottery information utility services on a worldwide basis became very attractive.

problems

The earliest lotteries encountered innumerable difficulties. New Hampshire and New York State lotteries, in particular, discovered how difficult were the problems of marketing, public relations, and financial control. The low sales volume experienced in the first year of operation led New York to authorize lottery ticket sales on a widespread, indiscriminate basis. With every corner newsstand and small store selling tickets, control became exceedingly difficult.

The height of frustration in New York was reached in December 1968, on a cold blustery day in lower Manhattan, when a dolly holding hundreds of thousands of ticket stubs was upset. The wind scattered the stubs in all directions, and a hundred workers chased them all over the Wall Street area. Thousands were never recovered, so, prior to a drawing, attempts were made to recreate the numbers of the missing stubs.

The problem, of course, was caused by the fact that lottery systems used two-part preprinted tickets, both parts bearing the same number. The "stub" part, bearing the purchaser's signature and address, was sent to the point of the lottery drawing and placed in a giant container with all of the other millions of tickets from all over the state.

The physical handling and control problems that arise from this system are very similar to those arising in the old style ticketing systems predating IU ticketing. Fraudulence is easy in a statewide physical ticket stub moving system. Errors and losses can and do occur frequently. The costs of accounting and control to provide a really tight system are staggering.

IU status

The lottery service described in this chapter did not exist anywhere in the world in 1968. The basic information utility concept described had not been designed in any detail, although New York State had received at least one proposal for such a service. The state government was giving serious consideration to a market and systems study by Ticket Reservation Systems, Inc. in early 1969. Several other states were also interested in the lottery IU during the late 1968–early 1969 period.

As has been the case with many other IU services, the system was technologically and economically feasible as early as 1966. The late 1960's and early 1970's will undoubtedly see the emergence of lottery service IU's, as various states become more and more frustrated with their manual ticket stub moving systems.

The most likely owners of the lottery IU's are the states. However, independent entrepreneurs may sweep the market by offering services to several or perhaps all states, as well as offering a national lottery service comparable to the English or Irish Sweepstakes.

the general concept

The basic concept in the lottery service IU is to substitute for preprinted tickets an electronic central inventory of all tickets. As in the ticketing IU, each lottery ticket seller will be supplied with a ticket printing terminal connected on line to the IU center. The lottery tickets will be printed on line as the purchaser pays for them. A record, by number, of tickets sold will be kept in the center. The numbers on the tickets and at the center will, of course, match under tight control of the IU program.

As the time for lottery drawings comes near, at the drawing location, the center prints out stubs properly numbered and identified as to which person or organization location sold it. These stubs can be printed in strip form and burst automatically, or printed individually and, untouched by human hands, fed directly into the drawing container. They can be automatically and mechanically shuffled and mixed thoroughly inside the container, insuring random distribution. If desirable, the central computers can spew the stubs into the container in a random numbering sequence.

The drawings can easily be held at several different locations throughout the state, because the stub printers can be connected on line to the IU center. The purchasing public can thus attend a drawing in their own locality periodically, and advance publicity about various drawings can be used to enhance ticket sales.

controls

The ticket seller, in this system, can be held responsible for keeping track of who purchased the tickets sold. Or, alternatively, a separate signed record can be mailed or otherwise delivered to the IU center. However, the big advantage of this service is the complete elimination of paper movement and control. So, it is likely that the game will be played only "by the numbers." The purchaser of the lottery ticket will be responsible for checking a published list of winning numbers in the newspapers or at the place where he bought the ticket. His name and address will probably not be recorded anywhere, and he will not be notified by the lottery if he wins. The central IU will supply a list of the winning numbers to all newspapers and other publications and will print the winning numbers at the locations where the tickets were sold, or will deliver notifications by mail.

Controls over cash in this system can be built into the terminals themselves. Since a continuously updated record of tickets sold is maintained at the IU for each selling terminal, the amount of cash due is also kept up to the minute. An invoicing system with on-line printouts of amounts due and reminder notices at each terminal can be made part of the service. Alternatively, a terminal cash clearing procedure using supervisory or collection personnel can be followed, again utilizing the on-line terminal in the procedure itself.

Audit trails and controls can easily be programmed into the central IU because of the on-line connection with every ticket selling point. In effect, no ticket can be sold without complete monitoring and control by the center.

Each terminal can be "watched" by the IU center and unusual activity detected. For example, an extremely high rate of ticket sales in a given period may indicate that a visit to the terminal is called for. Or the average rate of ticket sales for each terminal for specific hours of the day or days of the week can be measured. Any wide deviations from the normal patterns might call for a check.

advantages

The lottery service IU has the great advantage of eliminating the physical movement of ticket stubs. The problem created by the wind on Wall Street will never again arise. The costs of collecting, transporting, and keeping physical control over all of the ticket stubs are eliminated. The controls are provided by a powerful computing center capability combined with on-line monitoring.

Drawings can be controlled in a much better fashion and yet made more flexible and held more frequently and in more locations. The human element, with its capacity for errors, can be largely eliminated in the drawing procedure.

open questions

Two major questions have been raised by state lottery authorities about the type of IU service described herein. The first question is whether the purchasing public and the controlling authorities will accept a service that does not take the responsibility of notifying the winners directly.

The purchaser's signature and name and address appearing on the actual drawing stub has a particular psychological appeal that is difficult to replace. The substitutions suggested earlier, while far less costly than some compromise solution to this problem, nevertheless, may not be acceptable to the public. This factor may be more true in those states where the manual signed stub system has been in operation than in a state starting off with the IU lottery service. Public nonacceptance of the elimination of name and address notification may not mean nonacceptance of the lottery service IU. As was suggested earlier, a compromise could be reached, in which the ticket seller takes on the responsibility for keeping a name and address log for each purchaser.

For purchases made on credit no more extra work is created. In fact, as the SAVE information utility begins to function on a nationwide, or at least statewide basis, the SAVE card and system will automatically provide the required name and address information. The lottery ticket purchase will, of course, be a cash transaction, with the amount being transferred from the ticket purchaser's account to the ticket seller's account. With SAVE, the cash clearing operation between the IU and the ticket sellers also becomes very much simplified. There is only a periodic SAVE transfer of funds, less commission of course. All of this implies an online link between the SAVE center, where consumer names and addresses are stored, and the lottery service IU, where the numbers of the SAVE cards that purchased winning tickets are stored and looked up at the time of the drawings.

As the cost of CRT terminals with touch or light pen facilities comes down, a system for entering the ticket purchaser's name and/or identity with address being stored centrally may become feasible. This system will make use of the interactive ideas and displays described in Chapter 6 on PDS. If the purchaser's name is already in the system, and it would be if he had ever purchased a ticket before, the ticket seller will display his name and verify it through a series of screen touches, similar to finding an individual's file in PDS.

If his name is not in the center, the ticket seller will enter it by using the screen touch technique with keyboard displayed, under control of an interactive program that will minimize errors and speed up the name entry procedure.

If CRT terminals are used, the winning numbers and names can be displayed either by broadcast, or upon a request from the terminal. In this fashion, a ticket purchaser believing he has a winning ticket can go to the selling terminal where he bought it and ask the ticket seller to verify whether his number had won.

This process can even be extended to a payment authorization from seller to purchaser, in which funds will automatically be transferred from the lottery account into the ticket seller's account when the CRT terminal is triggered and authorization given for the seller to pay the purchaser his cash prize. SAVE will, of course, make this procedure even more feasible.

The second open question about IU service is a much more subtle one. Why not have the computer at the lottery IU center perform the drawings electronically? Now, any computer programmer or mathematician can tell you that it is possible to program a computer to make a completely random selection of numbers from the list of purchased ticket numbers stored in the IU memory.

The question is: will anybody believe it when the computer prints out the winning numbers it has selected at random? The answer is probably negative, not for many years to come. It is not so much a matter of belief that the computer programmers might have cheated (which could happen) but rather a psychological need for seeing all of those ticket stubs tumbling around in a barrel and an obviously honest, unbiased pretty girl reaching in pulling one out at random. However, if the computer selection were ever to be accepted, another major cost would be eliminated.

terminals

The types of terminals that the earliest lottery IU's use will probably closely resemble the ticketing service terminals described in Chapter 5. Certainly, the requirements for printing are quite similar. Continuous form stiff stock paper with a tightly controlled ticket number printing mechanism is required.

However, the keyboard will be considerably simplified. The only need for data entry is during the clearing process for accounting purposes. Of course, if the name and address compromise system is to be used, then a full alphanumeric keyboard or else a CRT terminal will be necessary. As mentioned above, the lowering cost of CRT terminals and their interactive advantages will probably cause a trend in that direction in future lottery IU's.

8 *tax service*

off-line tax computer services

In the mid-1960's, several computer based tax services were introduced on a national basis. The two best known services were Litton Industries' Datatax and Commercial Clearing House's Computax. The services were offered to tax advisors, tax consultants, lawyers, CPA's, and accounting firms engaged in assisting individuals and corporations in filing their income tax returns.

The off-line, batch processing services that were introduced accepted the standard tax forms filled out by the taxpayer and his advisor. These forms were keypunched at the tax computation center and cards entered into the computer. The service performed all computations from the raw data, checked on various aspects of the information provided on the form, printed out a final tax return form, and mailed this completed tax return back to the taxpayer's advisor.

problems

There were many problems with these off-line tax services. The usual programming and data collection/keypunching problems were encountered. Errors tended to crop up, or exceptions arose that the computer had no way of checking. In these cases, there was no alternative but to send the forms back to the tax advisor and ask for new entries. If the taxpayer was all the way across the country from the computer center, turnaround time using the mail service was too long.

The main problem, however, was the tremendous bottleneck that developed every year as April 15 rolled around. As the deadline for filing drew nearer, the total volume of tax forms grew larger, the turnaround time grew longer, and yet the pressure for fast response was greater as the time to file grew shorter. In effect, the entire system broke down during the first year or two of operation of all the services.

internal revenue service

At about the same time that the off-line computer tax services were appearing, the Internal Revenue Service undertook studies for a nationwide computer system of their own. The basic idea of the IRS system was to provide on-line terminals in every IRS regional and field office, connected to a central OLRT center in Washington. Directors of Internal Revenue and their staffs would be able to process the returns filed in their offices, checking computations, and making file inquiries in an on-line fashion.

This system was supplied by the General Electric Company and went into its first test operation at a regional office in Houston in late 1968. The operator at the CRT terminal can display the tax form on the screen and fill in the blanks from the taxpayer's form. Keying errors are thus controlled and minimized through the on-line, interactive technique. The resulting verified information is recorded on tape for later processing and record updating.

The system provides to the regional locations and field offices an inquiry and display capability. The offices can thereby answer taxpayers' questions promptly and minimize additional requests by IRS to taxpayers for information previously furnished.

Several of the states also have in the planning stages on line–real time systems for the handling of tax returns and for answering inquiries about corporate or individual tax status. In these cases, of course, state or local taxes are involved.

relationships among tax participants

To an independent observer, all of these separate tax computing and processing systems seem wasteful and inefficient. The same basic process seems to be repeated over and over again, using the same basic raw data. The taxpayer collects and organizes his tax return data. His advisor reviews it with him and helps fill out the tax return. Together they partially compute the final values and the details of the return. A tax computing service then completes the computations and makes various checks for accuracy and completeness. The tax return form may go through two or more cycles at this level if there are errors in it. Finally, the completed, signed tax return is sent to a district office of the IRS.

At the IRS office another transfer step is taken to change both the detailed data on the return as well as the final amounts into a form acceptable to the IRS computer system. Punched cards were used in an early phase; CRT terminals with keyboards, in a later phase. At IRS headquarters, the computations are again checked for accuracy and completeness, and compared with the taxpayer's past performance as well as with standards for his tax bracket and type.

If a state tax return is involved, the forms also go to the state center, if they have one, where the same processing takes place.

By this time, certain computations on the same basic initial data have taken place about five times. Furthermore, the information on the tax return has passed through a manual to computer format at least twice, and in some cases three or four times.

The interrelationships among all of the organizations and individuals involved, the overlaps in computations, the data processing, and the checking required at each step cause the independent observer to speculate on a national service available to all.

national tax service

The national tax service IU to be described herein does not exist. It results from the author's speculation on what is possible by utilizing the technology available in the late 1960's. It will be obvious from the description that many legal and business practice changes would be necessary for implementation of the service. The efficiencies to be gained and the savings that could be achieved on a national basis, as in the case of SAVE, should be staggering. The justifications for a national tax service should far outweigh the legal or political problems that would have to be solved.

From several points of view, the logical owner and operator of the service would be the Internal Revenue Service. However, the prevalent "big brother" fear of IRS and the desire on the part of IRS to retain an independent check on all taxpayers may dictate that some other organization own and operate the service.

In the description that follows, the latter assumption will be made. Without defining who it is, it will be assumed that the tax service IU is owned and operated by some completely independent organization, certified by the government, by the CPA's, by the SEC, and by anyone else who cares. Under this assumption, the IRS becomes just another subscriber, albeit a rather large one. State governments, local governments, CPA's and accounting firms, law firms, taxpaying corporations, and individual taxpayers would also be subscribers.

system description

An IU system will maintain tax records for IRS, and state and local governments on all taxpayers, individual and organizational, for the entire country. Past history records as well as current year information, names and current addresses, most recent tax status, data received from all sources on income, and other taxpayer status information will be stored.

The system may use a single central OLRT facility, or it may use a regional structure. The economics of the system design configuration will be dictated to some extent by the same considerations that were found in the SAVE network. A regional arrangement will be best if a very large percentage of the IU transactions for any given cluster of taxpayers tends to remain in a local or regional area.

Subscriber locations will be equipped with CRT terminals. The terminals will have either light-pen or screen-touch capabilities, plus keyboards and on-line printers. Likely subscriber locations are IRS district offices, IRS headquarters, state tax offices, city and county tax offices, CPA firm tax offices, law firm tax offices, accounting firms, tax consultants, and tax offices in large corporations. Individual taxpayers would go to one of the subscriber locations listed above in order to file their returns. Mail returns will still be possible for those who are unable to, or do not wish to, go to a location with a CRT terminal. The mailed returns will be processed at the nearest terminal in the same manner as those processed with the taxpayer present.

system operation

The case of an individual taxpayer using a CPA firm as tax advisor will be described first. Mr. Jones collects his raw data (W2 forms, deduction information, bills, receipts, check stubs, payment records, and tax returns for prior years) and goes to the office of the tax partner, Mr. Ross, handling his account in the CPA firm.

Jones and Ross sit down together in front of the CRT terminal on Ross' desk. Ross turns on the set and dials the number of the National Tax Service. When connected, the service displays a list of actions, and Ross points to "File on Individual Tax Return—Joint," since Jones is filing a joint return for him and his wife. Since Jones filed a joint return the year before, the service guides Ross through a short series of points at the screen and winds up displaying Jones' name, address, wife's name, and other information at the top of the tax form. (See Figure 8-1.)

Jones looks over the display, notes there are no changes since last year in his basic family data, and Ross points to "No Changes," an action box displayed on the CRT screen.

Form 1040 — U.S. Individual Income Tax Return 1968

U.S. Treasury Department, Internal Revenue Service

U.S. Individual Income Tax Return for the year January 1–December 31, 1968, or other taxable year beginning_____, 1968, ending_____, 19____

Please print or type

Harry T. and Julia P. Jones	**Your social security number** 249 03 6735
1425 Fifth Street	**Your occupation** Business Manager
Mandleville, New Hampshire, 21406	**Spouse's social security number** 248 72 1916

Enter below name and address used on your return for 1967 (if same as above, write "Same"). If none filed, give reason. If changing from separate to joint or joint to separate returns, enter 1967 names and addresses.
Same

Spouse's occupation Housewife

Your present employer and address **New Hampshire Spring Co., 110 East Avenue, Nashua, N.H. 21325**

Your Filing Status—check only one:

- 1a ☐ Single
- 1b ☒ Married filing joint return (even if only one had income)
- 1c ☐ Married filing separately. If spouse is also filing a return, enter her (his) social security number in space provided above and give first name here _____
- 1d ☐ Unmarried Head of Household
- 1e ☐ Surviving widow(er) with dependent child

Your Exemptions   Regular   65 or over   Blind

	Regular	65 or over	Blind	Enter number of boxes checked ▶
2a Yourself . . .	☒	☐	☐	
2b Spouse . . .	☒	☐	☐	2

3a First names of your dependent children *who lived with you* **John, Philip, Mary**

Enter number ▶ 3

3b Number of other dependents (from page 2, Part I, line 3)

4 Total exemptions claimed . . . . ▶ 5

Income

If joint return include all income of both husband and wife

5	Wages, salaries, tips, etc. If not shown on attached Forms W–2 attach explanation	5	
6	Other income (from page 2, Part II, line 8)	6	
7	Total (add lines 5 and 6)	7	*
8	Adjustments to income (from page 2, Part III, line 5)	8	
9	Total income ("adjusted gross income") (subtract line 8 from line 7)	9	*

Find tax from table —OR—

10	If you do not itemize deductions and line 9 is under $5,000, find tax in tables on pages 12–14 of instructions. Omit lines 11a, b, c, or d. **Enter tax on line 12a.**	10	
11a	If you itemize deductions, enter total from page 2, Part IV, line 17 If you do not itemize deductions, and line 9 is $5,000 or more enter the larger of: (1) 10 percent of line 9; **OR** (2) $200 ($100 if married and filing separate return) plus $100 for each exemption claimed on line 4, above. **Deduction under (1) or (2) limited to $1,000 ($500 if married and filing separately).**	11a	

Figure tax using tax rate schedules

11b	Subtract line 11a from line 9. Enter balance on this line	11b	*
11c	Multiply total number of exemptions on line 4, above, by $600	11c	3000 *
11d	Subtract line 11c from line 11b. Enter balance on this line. (Figure your tax on this amount by using tax rate schedule on page 11 of instructions.) **Enter tax on line 12a.**	11d	*

12a	Tax (Check if from: Tax Table ☐, Tax Rate Schedule ☐, Sch. D ☐, or Sch. G ☐)	12a	
12b	Tax surcharge. If line 12a is less than $734, find surcharge from tables on page 10 of instructions. If line 12a is $734 or more, multiply amount on line 12a by .075 and enter result. (If you claim retirement income credit, use Schedule B (Form 1040) to figure surcharge.)	12b	
12c	Total (add lines 12a and 12b)	12c	
13	Total credits (from page 2, Part V, line 4)	13	

Your Tax, Credits, and Payments

14a	Income tax (subtract line 13 from line 12c)	14a	*
14b	Tax from recomputing prior year investment credit (attach statement)	14b	
15	Self-employment tax (Schedule C–3 or F–1)	15	
16	Total tax (add lines 14a, 14b, and 15)	16	*
17	Total Federal income tax withheld (attach Forms W–2)	17	Make check or money order payable to Internal Revenue Service.
18	Excess F.I.C.A. tax withheld (two or more employers—see page 5 of instr.)	18	
19	☐ Nonhighway Federal gasoline tax—Form 4136, ☐ Reg. Inv.—Form 2439	19	
20	1968 Estimated tax payments (include 1967 overpayment allowed as a credit)	20	
21	Total (add lines 17, 18, 19, and 20)	21	*

Balance Due or Refund

22	If payments (line 21) are less than tax (line 16), enter **Balance Due. Pay in full with this return**	22	*
23	If payments (line 21) are larger than tax (line 16), enter **Overpayment**	23	*
24	Amount of line 23 you wish credited to 1969 Estimated Tax	24	*
25	Subtract line 24 from 23. Apply to: ☐ U.S. Savings Bonds, with excess refunded or ☐ Refund only	25	*

Under penalties of perjury, I declare that I have examined this return, including accompanying schedules and statements, and to the best of my knowledge and belief it is true, correct, and complete. If prepared by a person other than taxpayer, his declaration is based on all information of which he has any knowledge.

Sign here ▶

Your signature _____ Date _____

▶ Signature of preparer other than taxpayer _____ Date _____

Spouse's signature (If filing jointly, BOTH must sign even if only one had income) _____   Address _____

114

*Figure 8-1 (opposite page)   Cursor method
of completing a tax return on a CRT terminal.*

The result of this step is that, with no writing, printing, or key pressing, Jones and Ross, aided by the interactive capabilities of the service, have automatically placed in the central memory the following data for *this* year's tax return:

Taxpayer's name, spouse's name

Address or addresses

Social security numbers of taxpayer and wife

Employer's name

Number and type of dependents and names

Exemptions and filing status

Simultaneously, a "working" record is set up for Jones by the IU service. It contains the above information and a memory version of the tax form itself. The first page of this tax form is now displayed on the screen with the information above filled in and the rest of the lines displayed with blanks.

Ross and Jones are now ready to fill in the blanks, beginning with income. They do so by one of two methods. The first method is to type in the numbers from the keyboard of the terminal or by pointing to numbers on a simulated keyboard displayed on the screen. A moving cursor flashes underneath the place in the blank space where the next numerical character will be inserted. The cursor moves only where the blanks are located. (See Figure 8-1.) The only numbers typed in are the raw data figures, such as salary and deductions. The figures that can be derived by computations are automatically computed and displayed at each step of the procedure. These figures are marked by asterisks in the tax form illustrated.

The second method is to rely on the tax service to display a series of choices for the value of the figure being inserted in the blank. By pointing to a series of ranges, Ross can tell the service what Jones' salary was, without ever actually touching a key. For example, assume Jones' salary for the year before was $18,575.00. The service would first

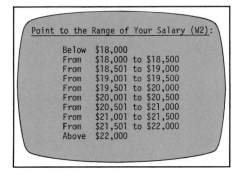

*First
CRT screen
display*

display some salary range choices near this level and above it, under the assumption that Jones might be receiving the same salary this year or a moderate raise. Then Jones and Ross would see something the first display shows.

Assuming Jones' salary for this year was $20,305, representing a relatively normal ten percent raise, Ross points to the sixth line from the top: "From $20,001 to $20,500." Jones and Ross see the second display. Ross points to the seventh line from the top: "$20,301 to $20,350," and the screen shows the third display. Ross points to the top line: "$20,301 to $20,305," and the screen shows the fourth display of the series. Ross points to the bottom line, "$20,305," and, in four points at the screen, the salary to the nearest dollar has been entered.

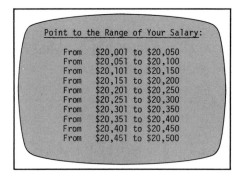

*Second
CRT screen
display*

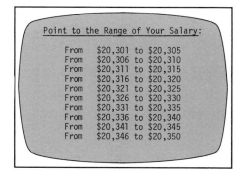

*Third
CRT screen
display*

In a similar fashion, other figures can be entered, where the service initiates a series of displays with dollar ranges based on last year's tax return values.

The service next displays the deductions page of the tax form. As Jones and Ross begin to work on deductions, they can request a display of last year's items for reference purposes. The service also provides a reminder list of various kinds of deductions in each category and summaries of the same type found in the instructions on the tax form. The reminders take the form of displayed questions. For example, the screen may show the fifth display illustrated. As each item is considered, the service provides interactive computational assistance, tables, suggested standard values for various items, and a kind of scratch-pad, note-taking surface on the CRT screen. For example, when sales taxes

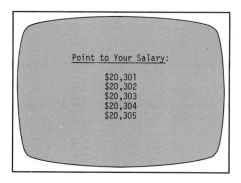

*Fourth
CRT screen
display*

117

*Fifth
CRT screen
display*

are entered, the tax rates for the taxpayer's resident state and any nearby states where he may have made purchases are shown. A computational formula is displayed that permits Ross to enter the gross amounts spent in each pertinent state, and the resultant total sales tax for all purchases is computed.

The service continually checks deductions for compliance with tax regulations and compares every item with standards and averages for Jones' class of taxpayer. It also compares them with Jones' own deductions over the past few years. If any item falls outside limits set by the system, too high or too low in the comparisons, the service calls this discrepancy to the attention of Jones and Ross. This action, in effect, is an in-advance substitute for a review by a tax man in an IRS office.

At the end of the procedure, the entire form as it has been completed is displayed to both Ross and Jones for final review. If they are satisfied, they inform the tax service that Jones is officially filing the tax return as it is in central memory and as displayed. They press a "Print" button on the terminal twice and receive two copies of the form as it has appeared on the screen, one for Jones and one for Ross. The official, legal tax return for the IRS is now the stored information in the IU. The IRS could, if desired, request a printout of Jones' return at any time.

The method for making the stored information legal will require an acceptable substitute for the signatures of the taxpayer, his spouse, and his advisor. Future technology may permit the signing of the form as it is displayed on the screen, and the storing and redisplay along with printing of the signature. However, at an earlier date, a substitute, such as an identity card, inserted in the terminal will probably be acceptable. Obtaining the spouse's signature equivalent may be somewhat more difficult.

By extension of this operational description, it can be visualized how the state and local tax returns will be filed. Since most of the raw data for them is derived from the federal return, very little new information has to be put in.

As tax returns are filed, the tax collectors (federal, state, and local) can gain access to all of the returns upon demand or as an automatic by-product of the filing procedure. If IRS or the states still retain their own computer systems, on-line links to the national tax service IU can provide up-to-the-minute reporting and accounting.

economies

The economies of the system described should be obvious. No paper is generated or mailed or otherwise moved around. The copies retained by the taxpayer and his advisor are merely filed for future reference. The keypunching and other costs associated with transforming paper tax returns to computer format are eliminated. All of the overlapping computing, checking, and double checking of the return is eliminated. The final return is completed in one session, while the taxpayer is present. The reduction in delay and the saving in time and effort for both the taxpayer and his advisor are substantial.

Of course, the organizations currently supplying tax computation services in an off-line fashion will be out of business. It is presumed that some of them may wish to become the unidentified owner and operator mentioned at the beginning of this postulation.

part iii   design

Part iii is a semitechnical section of the book, directed at lay readers who wish to do more than just skim the surface of information utility technology. It discusses the various aspects and components of utility design in a manner useful to beginning designers, and understandable to using subscribers, owners, operators, financiers, and the lay public.

The components discussed are: central computer and storage hardware, communications hardware and systems, terminals (remote input-output hardware), software, controls, and systems design considerations. Advanced designers may also find the overview of interest, although other sources will be more useful for detailed design techniques.

9 *design considerations*

The designer of an IU begins with the same set of considerations necessary for any on line–real time system and then adds a new list peculiar to IU's in general as well as to his own particular one. OLRT design considerations have been covered in depth in prior publications.[1] This chapter will focus on considerations unique to IU's, both in equipment and software areas as well as in overall systems design.

The level of systems design complexity for an IU can be said to be two levels above the batch processing system and one level more complex than an OLRT system. Three main contributing factors cause this higher level of complexity over an ordinary OLRT system. The first is the wider variety of transactions generated by a large number of different types of subscribers in different organizations. The second is the absolute necessity of record and transaction isolation and protection when many organizations, often competitive, are tied into the same system. The third is the increased desirability and necessity in many IU's for interactive two-way communication between subscriber and system.

In the typical OLRT system, self-contained within a single organization, a user generates simple transactions, selected from a well-defined limited list, and seldom becomes involved in a complicated series of interactions with the system. In the extreme case of an IU such as PDS, the user generates completely unexpected unformulated transactions, in which each one becomes intertwined with, and dependent on, a series of transactions that have occurred previously. At the same time, the system must deal with hundreds of other users generating their own series of interactions. The complexity implied, especially in software, to keep track of all this interaction is obvious.

1. See Sprague, *Electronic Business Systems*, Chapter 4, 5, and 10.

equipment

The equipment required for IU's falls into the same three general categories as for any OLRT system: central processing and storage, data communications, and terminals. With only a few exceptions, the design considerations for central processing and storage are similar to those for any large scale OLRT system.

Storage & Retrieval Equipment   The increased number of transactions and the much wider variety of types in an IU places a burden on the conventional central processing and storage designs and will undoubtedly bring about some fundamental hardware and software design changes. The burden on software is particularly demanding. The bottleneck in processing always turns out to be memory access rate—*not* access time, but rate. A detailed analysis of this problem and a proposed solution called ISAR were accomplished by Jaap Unk.[2] The University of Utah and General Electric Company initiated a research program to explore the concept in 1967. The name was changed to SAFORS.

Briefly, the SAFORS concept involves shifting the burden of memory storage and retrieval functions, including program as well as data storage, onto a subsystem that contains its own logic. (See Figure 9-1.) In fact, it contains its own stored program computer whose job is to keep track of, monitor, and control all requests for memory accesses from the main IU processor or processors.[3]

The IU processors send requests for memory accesses, which include searching plus reading or writing, to SAFORS in content defined structure. For example, a request may be as complex as this: "Please find the individual's file on Joe Smith and change his home phone number to 314-8461, and tell me when you have accomplished this task." SAFORS

2. J. M. Unk, *ISAR Information Storage and Retrieval.* 3 pamphlets published by ISYS in The Hague, Holland, 1964.
3. "Processor" in this context refers to equipment, not software.

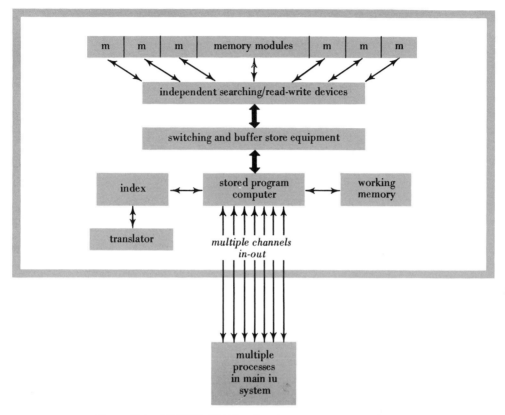

Figure 9-1   SAFORS (ISAR) subsystem.

translates this into its own language, looks into its index (which may be in a memory module but is shown separately in Figure 9-1), goes to the file, makes the change, checks it, and sends back an OK to the IU.

In effect, much of the software burden on the main IU processors is thus removed and replaced by a mixture of hardware and software in SAFORS.[4] The multiple searching-reading-writing devices in SAFORS can all be working simultaneously on different memory modules. In addition, as shown by the variations in spacing of the devices, varying

---

4. The software may be "firmware," the new term for fixed stored logic programs.

size pieces of memory may be set up by grouping modules and assigned to the searching devices as a function of access frequency to the particular group. A common characteristic of all IU's is that a frequency of access distribution resembling the Poisson curve is found spread across the entire memory. As many as 90 per cent of the memory accesses can sometimes occur in as little as 10 or 20 per cent of the memory.

Thus, a key feature of this new system design philosophy is to produce a much closer match between access distribution in the memory itself, and the actual requirements generated by IU transactions.

Evaluation by the systems designer of this new approach will be complicated, because it involves hardware-software tradeoffs that strike at the heart of the general purpose-stored program computer market. Resistance to the concept on the part of software groups within the main frame part of the computer industry has been and will probably continue to be great.

Data Communications The principal differences in IU data communication considerations, compared to other OLRT systems, will be stimulated by the eventual desirability of placing terminals in every conceivable location where human beings can be found. This implies a network as vast as the combined telephone, teletype, radio, television, and power networks. Furthermore, the costs must be very low, and the convenience of being connected at any point, very high.

One way to achieve these objectives is to devise ways and means of "riding on" the existing networks. AT & T, in particular, has for more than a decade been attacking the problem of superimposing data communications on top of its vast voice network. This study has three implications for IU systems designers.

First, they can consider standard "dial up" techniques, using the public telephone network for establishing a data communications connection at voice grade transmission rates (2000–3000 bits per second) between their subscriber's terminals and the IU center. Dialing is generally much less expensive for a normal subscriber than any private voice grade service. It is also a facility available at many more, in fact nearly all, desirable fixed locations.

Secondly, the designer can consider the use of the telephone instrument itself, particularly the touch tone phone, with twelve instead of ten buttons, as a terminal, or as part of a terminal. Since the same phone can be used for both voice and data transmission, costs are inherently lower. The telephone and the public network also have one very convenient characteristic that most other terminals and data communications systems do not have. Voice substitution for data or information is easy. A voice reply to an inquiry generated by a digital-to-voice converter at the IU can send back the oral information over the public network to any telephone. The same phone can be used to generate the digital touch tone transaction that initiated the inquiry.[5]

Before the end of the century, the reverse of this situation will be developed. IU centers will be equipped to recognize subscriber's voices and oral information spoken by them, so that two-way voice communications between subscriber and IU centers will be possible.

The third implication of using the public phone network is that the IU designer can consider acoustically coupled terminals for portable subscriber situations.[6] Prior to the development of voice input, understood by the IU computer in its raw form, there will be portable terminals of various types acoustically coupled to any telephone, including pay phones. In the not too distant future, a very small, lightweight, battery operated CRT with acoustical coupling will give the executive access to his PDS services from the airport pay phone (which is where he seems to be a good share of the time).

The acoustically coupled terminal situation was resisted for a long time by AT & T, but the judgment of the FCC in

---

5. This technique is called DIVA by AT & T for Digital Input Voice Answer.
6. *Acoustical coupling* is the term applied to the placement of a sound generating device over the mouthpiece of the standard telephone and transmitting either voice or touch tone signals.

the Hushaphone case began to turn the tide in this direction in 1968.

There are other communications considerations associated with the differences in facilities and tariffs between local private lines, private long line, TWX, TELEX, high speed facilities like Telpac, and tariff structures like WATS and INWATS. A complete book could be written on these subjects for OLRT systems.[7] Some of them will be touched upon later in this chapter, under IU network design considerations.

Terminals Of the three equipment categories, terminals are the most important for IU systems design because of their wide variety and because they represent the IU as far as the subscriber is concerned. "The IU service is no better than the terminal" is a cardinal design rule. If the housewife likes a green phone in the kitchen and a pink one in the bedroom, that is what she gets. If the harassed executive cannot stand noisy typing in his office, he gets a silent printer.

Two points of view regarding terminal designs seemed to grow out of the OLRT and time sharing eras of the 1950's and 1960's. The first view was that general purpose terminals, like the standard teletype machine or telephone instrument or CRT with typewriter keyboard, would serve most subscriber purposes. The second view was that tailor-made terminals for individual subscriber applications are best. As always, the most significant factor in this choice was cost. Since terminal costs in early IU's made up more than one third of the total system hardware cost, unit terminal prices were all important.

However, also of significance in the choice are error control, ease of subscriber use and consequently easier marketing efforts, compatibility with available lowest cost communications facilities, degree of interaction between subscriber and IU, complexity and variety of transactions, and compatibility with or combining with OLRT terminals the subscriber uses within his own system.

7. See Sprague, *Electronic Business Systems*, Chapter 5.

As mentioned in earlier chapters, in the industry oriented IU's a limited amount of interaction is required and a limited, rather well-defined, set of transaction types have become standard. In these cases, such as airline reservation services, savings bank and savings & loan services, stock quotation services, etc., tailor-made terminals became prevalent. Compatibility with standard OLRT systems, which already used tailored terminals in these industries, was essential. On the other hand, nearly all problem solving (time sharing) utilities started with, and still use, general purpose terminals.

example of tailored terminal

As an illustration of a tailored terminal, the design of the ticket reservation services terminal will be described. (Refer to Figure 5-1.) In the TRS situation, as was pointed out in Chapter 5, a special printer is required in the terminal to print tickets on stiff paper ticket stock. Preprinted continuous ticket strips are essential to conserve print time. Color stripes for coding purposes will be demanded by subscribers who stick with tradition. Speeds faster than typical teletype or electric typewriter speeds are essential.

In addition, a tailor-made keyboard will be designed to facilitate entry of ticket sales and inquiry descriptions. Columns of keys are used to reduce errors and speed up key pressing. The columns are divided into groups for date of performance, time of day, type of event, type of seats desired, number of seats, and type of transaction. The types of transactions are sell, check availability, check first available performance, and hold. Tailor-made displays and special printing responses will be designed to answer the various transaction types.

This is seemingly a ready-made situation for a tailor-made terminal. However, as pointed out in Chapter 5, continuous interactive requirements in complex seat selling situations, may make a general purpose CRT highly desirable as a replacement for the keyboard, the special displays, and part of the printing response. The ticket printer will obviously continue to be special.

example of general purpose terminal

The PDS terminal is a true general purpose device from the equipment design standpoint. The executive's terminal is a standard CRT with light pen. If he has a printer attached, it will be a standard silent type of fast printer. The secretary's terminal is a standard CRT with standard typewriter keyboard plus light pen and printer.

The technique that permits completely unstructured data entry and retrieval through a general purpose terminal by absolute amateurs is to make the terminal *appear to be tailor-made* at every step of every interaction. This can be done by displaying on the CRT screen a tailor-made keyboard, different at every step. The executive, in pointing to the screen, is, in effect, pressing groups of tailor-made keys to specify what he wants. The service interprets his pointings by using software in a manner analogous to the hardware interpretations of button pushings.

Figure 9-2   Twelve-button touch tone telephone keyboard. The two extra keys permit the generation of alphabetic data.

probable changes in terminal design and philosophy

The concept of creating whatever keyboard one chooses on the face of a CRT and then allowing someone to "press the keys" by pointing to them is bound to have the long-range effect of nearly eliminating tailor-made keyboards.

Furthermore, hardware implementation of tailored keyboards becomes difficult because of the limited meanings that can be assigned to any individual key. Codes must be used or remembered. In some cases, plastic overlays are placed over the keyboard to change the meaning of the keys. How much easier it will be when the highly interactive CRT with light pen, backed up by sophisticated software, becomes inexpensive. Then it will be possible to display a full keyboard on the screen and actually show in exact English, or with pictures if desirable, the true, full meaning of each key with no codes required. And a completely different keyboard will be displayed with the next interaction if called for.

other future terminals

The section of this chapter dealing with communications has already mentioned several new types of terminals or terminal design approaches. These are:

1. *Twelve-button touch tone phone.* The two extra buttons permit alphabetic data to be generated. One approach is to press one of the upper nine buttons followed by zero or one of the two extra buttons or a combination of them to designate which of the three letters always appearing on the button was desired. (See Figure 9-2.) For example, pressing the "2" key followed by the "α" key would transmit an A. Pressing the "2" key followed by the "β" key would transmit a C. A "2" followed by a zero would send a B. In this mode, some other action would have to switch the code to numeric. This might be pressing "1" followed by α, a combination which has no letter meaning.

2. *Acoustically coupled terminals.* These could be any of the types mentioned so far, with devices attached that convert the digital signals to the same touch tone audio signals one hears when touch tone keys are pushed. (See Figure 9-3.)

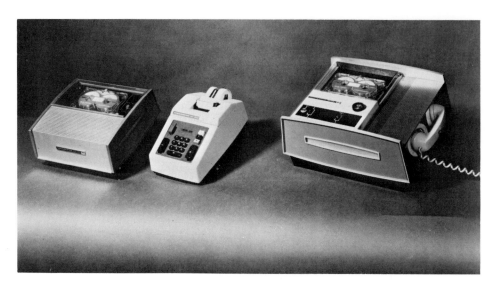

*Figure 9-3   Acoustically coupled terminal.
(Courtesy Digitronics Corporation,
Albertson, Long Island)*

Figure 9-4   A secretary using a CRT terminal.

*Figure 9-5   An engineer using a CRT
terminal in a laboratory.*

3. *DIVA*. This is actually just the terminal 1 above with voice answerback added.

4. *VIVA*. This would be a normal telephone with voice input as well as voice output.[8]

5. *Portable CRT*. This lightweight, battery operated, pocket or briefcase size CRT could be acoustically coupled to any telephone. (See Figures 9-4 and 9-5.)

8. An engineering prototype of a voice recognition system capable of recognizing a limited number of voices and a limited number of words spoken by these voices was tested at Mellonics Corporation in 1967.

information utility network design

Table 2-1 in Chapter 2 showed that some IU's are inherently local in nature, i.e., confined to a single community or metropolitan area. Others are obviously national in scope, and some may be regional, i.e., covering a state or a portion of the country. Many of the national IU's are listed as falling into all three categories.

A local IU will follow a network design pattern that is fairly simple and straightforward from the communications design point of view. Radial private lines will extend outward from the center, either to all terminals or to bunches of terminals served by a communications device. Another alternative may allow public dialing from all terminals, either on a per call basis or polling using WATS, or terminal originated calls using INWATS.[9]

However, a national IU has some interesting network design problems. Several alternatives, available in the local-regional-national network patterns, might be chosen. The completely centralized approach uses one information center and a data communications network something like the local IU to reach all of the subscriber terminals. Unfortunately, the radial private line to every terminal makes this alternative prohibitively expensive. As a result, special communications equipment and systems have been developed, so that private lines can still be used but shared among many stations and terminals. One example of such a system is Simulcom, developed by Ultronics Corporation for use in brokerage IU's. Most national IU's that operate on a centralized basis use the public telephone or teletype networks and utilize WATS or INWATS.

The second alternative for a national IU is to centralize selected processing and transactions and to handle other transactions from satellite centers in local communities or

9. The AT & T INWATS billing service allows any number of calls to be initiated by a specified list of phones in an area for a flat rate per month. WATS charges a flat rate, but the calls must originate at the center.

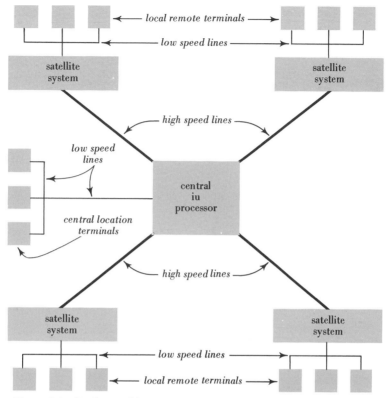

Figure 9-6   Design of IU satellite system.

regions around the country. The satellites resemble the local IU as far as terminals in their area and communications links are concerned. However, transactions requiring central action are passed by the satellite over a high speed private line to the IU center, and the response travels over the reverse path. (See Figure 9-6.)

Examples of this network design approach are the Ultronics and Bunker-Ramo stock quotation services. The satellites actually contain a continuously updated copy of selected stock information accumulated and processed in the center. Thus, the satellites are able to answer most queries on a local basis.

What the network designer is really doing in this approach is trading off communications savings for storage and some processing costs at the satellite. If simple inexpensive hardware can handle the job and if a large percentage of transactions can be handled locally it will save money.

The third alternative is to link together by private lines a network of local and/or regional IU's, each of which handles the bulk of transactions in its own area and once in a while passes on a transaction to some other center. The prime examples of this type of network will be the national credit information utility and its successor, SAVE. In this network, the nature of the utility is such that inter-communications among subscribers and the center in a community are voluminous, but the national transactions are small in number. Also, each data base is different. It is not necessary or desirable for all subscribers nationally to have access to the same data.

software considerations

Most of the special characteristics and requirements of IU's mentioned in the introduction to this chapter have a much greater impact on software design than on equipment design. Itemizing these requirements again, we find, when compared to standard OLRT systems, that they include:

1. Larger numbers of subscribers and more subscribers from different organizations

2. Wider varieties of transaction types

3. Subscriber interactive programming and program debugging

4. Simultaneous programming and nonprogramming transactions

5. Necessity for absolute record and program protection

6. Necessity for guaranteed isolation among various subscribers' data

7. Necessity for fast response in highly interactive services

8. Need to keep track of a trail of subscriber transactions, all interrelated in a series of interactions between the subscriber and the IU service

9. Need for accounting controls and audit trails in financially oriented services (such as SAVE and TRS)

10. Complex record keeping of subscriber file usage and transaction volumes in order to bill for IU services

11. Systems of interlocks to prevent unauthorized users from gaining access to particular records

12. Provisions for fallback and restoration in the event of equipment failures

13. Subscriber oriented applications packages, flexible enough to meet majority of demands, yet modular, relatively inexpensive, and easily marketable.

No single IU, with the possible exception of the general purpose type discussed in Chapter 3, has all of these special characteristics simultaneously. The software design considerations and the various techniques developed to meet the various requirements will therefore be quite different depending on the type of utility. As a result, no attempt will be made herein to describe any one utility's software. Rather, some general principles and the tricks of the software trade that have been used to solve some of the problems will be discussed.

superlanguages

The "executive" program or "operating systems" of the standard OLRT system or the multiprogramming batch systems are generally not capable enough to handle IU software requirements. A super-level language has been used in some IU's to control the entire structure. If programming and non-programming subscribers are both using the IU center simultaneously, a superlanguage is essential.[10]

What happens is that the superlanguage keeps track of and supervises an interpolating language unique to the IU and unknown to the subscribers. This interpolating language

10. The term *programming subscriber* as used here is not restricted to the conventional type of programmer-problem solver but could include engineers using graphical or analytical equivalents of program steps. It includes *any* subscriber creating a new type of transaction that was not IU preprogrammed.

receives all transactions or programs from subscribers in whatever language they might be using and executes each transaction with step-by-step checking and interlocks among memory sections. If a subscriber program contains a "bug," the interpolating language rejects the transaction and tells the subscriber what he did wrong, or at least gives him some clues. At every step of every transaction from every subscriber, the interpolating language checks *all* memory accesses, especially write commands, to see whether the subscriber involved has the right to gain access to that part of the IU's memory or not. It can also decide whether the subscriber has the right to *change* that part of the memory or not, even if he has access rights to it.

The superlanguage keeps an index and assigns memory segments to all subscribers for both programs and data. It knows at all times who can gain access to or change what. It also knows where in the IU's overall memory, each subscriber's information can be found, and it continuously allocates memory according to needs and service charges; i.e., a subscriber may pay more for faster memory than for slower less expensive memory.

Thus, a programming subscriber cannot "clobber" records or programs that do not belong to him through an inadvertent programming error. Nor can any subscriber gain access to any records he has no authorization to obtain. Furthermore, machine failures immediately throw the superprogram into a fail-safe procedure to protect and restore data and programs.

passwords and terminal identity

The techniques most widely used for interlocking records and for instructing the superlanguage as to who has authorization to gain access to what records are called the *password concept* and the *terminal identity technique*.

Each subscriber terminal *can* be equipped with a built-in, non-changeable (by the subscriber) identification code. The code can be transmitted to the IU with every transaction.

Thus, the IU software knows what terminal it is handling and can govern its memory allocation and access rules accordingly.

However, in many types of IU services such a scheme is impractical, either because the terminal is used by different subscribers, or else because it is a general purpose terminal, not under the complete control of the IU. An example of the latter would be a standard teletype machine or telephone or a portable acoustically coupled terminal.

In these cases, the password concept can be used. The subscriber identifies himself to the IU at the start of a period of use of a terminal by entering a password known only to him and the IU superlanguage. It can be any word or number he chooses, and it is stored by the superlanguage in the master subscriber index. It becomes associated with the subscriber's records, files, programs, and transactions, so that only upon use of the password is anyone authorized to gain access to any of them. The subscriber, in this system, can then use any terminal as long as he uses his password. He can, of course, give the password to others, for example, his secretary. If so, he bears the responsibility for what may happen. He can also change the password at any time by first using the old one to gain access, and then a special password-changing transaction. He may wish that any change be made only from his own special terminal.

In fact, combinations of terminal identity and passwords can be used to gain even tighter authorization protection. For example, the boss may use one password from his own terminal but prevent his secretary from using that same password from *her* terminal. Physical locks can also be provided for terminals, so that no one except keyholders can activate them.

A hierarchy of passwords can be set up, so that access to a broad variety of records is authorized for one group of users, while access to selected records requires knowledge of two passwords, and authorization to *change* a record requires knowledge of three passwords. An example may be in a SAVE corporate subscriber where access for automated bill paying and payroll transfers using the first password is given to a large group of employees. Budget planning records access is authorized by a second password issued to the executive group, but ability to change the budget plan may be limited by a third password to the president and treasurer.

indexes and memory allocation

As implied above, the superlanguage keeps track of where everything is located in memory and also keeps track of available empty memory. If we assume at least two levels of memory access speeds (for example, drums and discs), the superlanguage also keeps track of memory usage by subscriber and types of transactions and dynamically allocates memory modules according to access rate and time requirements, updating its available and used memory space indexes at the same time. Of course, the SAFORS subsystem mentioned earlier in this chapter will take much of this burden off of the IU superlanguage.

The indexes may be centralized or decentralized, i.e., spread throughout the various memory levels. For example, the gross subscriber allocating index may be kept in core storage, while the translating or computing indexes to find groups of records or programs for a given subscriber may be in drum storage, and the final index to reach the individual record may be in disc storage. In this case, each index leads or points to the memory location of the next.

chaining

As a subscriber's files and records become more voluminous and interrelated, the IU needs to relieve the subscriber of the burden of keeping track of record links. A technique called *chaining* or *ring structures* becomes useful in this situation. Chapter 6 on PDS mentioned the GE Microplex system, which consists of a series of linked rings of records. The term "ring" is used because each record of a given type (for example, individuals) contains an index address for the next record in the group. The last record contains the address of the first, thus forming a ring chain.

In this system, each record can be stored *anywhere* in memory, and the software finds a record by entering the ring at any point and then circling around it until it comes to the correct record. The linking of rings is used to jump from one kind of record (for example, individuals) to another kind that is related (for example, organizations to which the individuals belong).

Thus, a series of rings (for example, for individuals, organizations, and events) can keep track of and search for all of the interrelationships. In this case, the relationships would be: which individuals are members of which organizations, which individuals and organizations were involved in a series of events, etc. Given, for example, the approximate date and time of an event, and knowing that one individual and one organization were involved, an IU user can discover the event itself by searching around the event ring and linking it with the individual and organization rings until the intersection of all three is reached.

Chaining simplifies the indexing job because only the location of the beginning item in the chain needs to be indexed in detail.

packages

Perhaps the most complex software consideration is the determination, on a marketable and yet profit making basis, what software applications packages to make available initially, and how to add more as subscribers demand more.

The problem solving programming IU seems at first to have the easiest decision to make in this regard. All of its subscribers prepare their own packages. On the other hand, every one of them would like to use a different programming language, so the IU is faced with deciding what languages to make available. Tables 3-1 and 3-2 show what a large variation is possible in the available languages.

Actually, the industry oriented IU in which the bulk of the subscribers have very similar transaction requirements (whether they believe this or not) has by far the easiest software package decisions to make. The best example is MEDAC, in which nearly all doctors bill exactly the same way. Yet, even MEDAC has had packaging and marketing problems.

The worst example is the general purpose IU. It seems somewhat ironic that Keydata Corporation, the first general purpose IU and one of the earliest IU's of any kind, should have been faced with the most severe problems in software, and yet that is exactly what happened. The decisions as to which industries or which types of service to offer first and which software applications packages to offer to these initial subscribers were complex. Even more complex were the decisions about which packages to add to the initial ones, how to add them while subscribers were already using the IU, and how to price each new service.

Coupled with the severe software design considerations were severe marketing problems. Of course, now that IU's have become commonplace, marketing problems are perhaps different but not as severe.

No handy formula can be given for the solutions to all of these software applications problems. Each IU must develop its own approaches as it moves along. The PDS growth approach in software design, for example, will be markedly different from the airline reservation or the hotel service cases.

10 owners, operators, and regulatory implications

The federal government, the big computer companies, the big communications companies, the large service bureau operators, and the public in general all want to know who will own and operate the information utilities and whether or not they will be regulated. There are a number of interesting and important questions to be asked in this area. Not all of them will be answered by the Federal Communications Commission's hearings, which began in 1966 and are still not concluded.

Some of these questions are:

1. What organizations can, or should, or will be permitted to own information utilities?

2. Since owners and operators may not be the same organizations, who can, or should, or will be permitted to operate IU's?

3. Will IU's be regulated by the federal government?

4. If so, how and by what departments: FCC, the Justice Department, Comptroller of the Currency, Federal Reserve, Department of Commerce, Congress, National Science Foundation, Bureau of Standards, SEC, or some special newly created agency?

5. What monopolistic tendencies exist in an IU and how far will an owner be permitted to go?

6. What local agencies will be involved in regulation: utility commissions, state banking controllers, specially created local governmental agencies, etc.?

7. What are the emerging competitive factors leading toward or away from ownership?

8. Who will audit IU's and how will they be audited?

9. How can an owner forecast profits and competition?

10. What resources should an IU owner possess?

historical trends

Before we attempt to answer any or all of these questions, it would be wise to examine the history of ownership of IU's. A quick scanning of Tables 2-2, 3-1, 3-2, and 3-3 will show that, as of 1968, when these tables were last updated, a wide distribution of owner organizations had emerged. Perhaps the largest single type, if it can indeed be called that, was made up of private entrepreneurs. Universities formed the largest classification under operators, principally because, numerically, time sharing IU's predominated.

A list of types of owners and operators might include the following:

1. Independent or private proprietors
2. Government agencies
3. Universities
4. Commercial banks
5. Computer manufacturers
6. Communications companies
7. Industry groups
8. Large companies in an industry servicing parts of the industry. (For example, The Provident Institute for Savings, servicing savings institutions in Boston)
9. Computer service bureaus
10. Large electronic systems companies
11. Software companies
12. Community ownership—collections of organizations
13. Professional or trade associations or societies

An examination of how some of the IU's came into existence will help explain the ownership. The general purpose problem solving types had their genesis largely at universities. The Advanced Research Projects Agency (ARPA) of the Department of Defense was largely responsible for financially initiating the early IU's. Since ARPA funds were more readily assignable to universities and since universities had both the professional talent for IU development and

the immediate subscriber needs on campus, universities became the prime testing ground.

MIT and Dartmouth were notable pioneers. The exception to this university domination was System Development
Corporation, a nonprofit large electronic systems organization. ARPA funds and SDC ingenuity spawned several
different IU's, and SDC became an owner along with the
universities.

Major computer manufacturers realized that time sharing
was here to stay, and they supported university IU's, notably
GE at Dartmouth, and SDS at California, as well as initiating
general purpose problem solving IU's of their own.

Meanwhile, in earlier developments several companies
had spent a lot of time and money designing and installing
their own OLRT systems. These organizations discovered
they could offer a service to other companies in the same
business with very little additional investment and help pay
for their own initial investment.

The chief example of this development was the savings
bank service. Several of the first large savings banks and
savings and loan associations began offering service from
their own OLRT system to other savings institutions in the
same city or state. Thus, they automatically became IU
owners. In some cases, notably Provident Institute for Savings in Boston (Burroughs) and the Bank for Savings in New
York (NCR), the computer manufacturer who supplied the
system assisted in converting it to an IU and even became
part owner. Later, the computer manufacturers started their
own savings institution IU's.

The trend in some industry oriented IU's, such as the
stock brokerage field, was for systems oriented organizations like Bunker-Ramo, Ultronics, or Scantlin Electronics,
who were already selling many services and much equipment
to the industry, to become the natural owners of the IU's.

In other industry cases, groups of organizations or their
trade associations decided to band together for joint ownership of IU's to serve the entire industry or the firms in a

community. Examples of this trend are the group of hospitals in Indianapolis who own IHDA, a hospital service IU, and the network of credit IU's created and owned by Associated Credit Bureaus of America and their members.

The role of communications companies in the IU ownership picture depends heavily on the outcome of the FCC hearings. Western Union is on public record as intending to take an aggressive role in IU ownership. They have taken the position that either they should be permitted to compete for IU business without regulation, or else *all* IU owners should be regulated by the FCC.

AT & T has shown both technical and marketing indications that they would like to play a leading role in IU ownership because of their tremendous advantage in owning most of the communications network for IU's as well as many of the potential terminals (telephones). However, AT & T, operating under a consent decree, has not taken a public position on IU ownership. They could certainly, if unregulated, take over many, if not most, of the national IU's, just by sheer force of financial, technical, and operating control.

Computer manufacturers, in general, have not been as aggressive as might have been expected in becoming IU owners. The major exception is GE. There are some hidden marketing reasons for this situation. A computer manufacturer, by and large, is selling "main frames."[1] The sales commission structure, marketing policy and history, and the antitrust influence, especially in at least one case (IBM), keeps the marketing organization and the computer manufacturer top management from making a true substantial commitment to offering IU services. In the one case, Service Bureau Corporation, a wholly owned subsidiary of IBM, has become an IU with national scope, and IBM has transferred all of their IU services (Quiktran, Datatext, and the Dun and Bradstreet Industry Information Service) to SBC.

Commercial banks would also seem to be likely IU

1. *Main frame* is a computer industry term for the general purpose computer to be found at the center of any system.

owners. The reasons have to do with the possible expansion of bank services to include financial and money handling services, in addition to the wide variety of computer based services already offered by banks. The bank will be the most likely candidate for ownership of SAVE, for example. However, with exception of a few isolated IU's owned by banks, such as MEDAC, and the St. Louis savings service, this trend has yet to begin. Perhaps one of the reasons is natural bank conservatism, but certainly the lack of any real concerted commercial bank efforts toward their own OLRT systems is the strongest negative factor.

As mentioned in the beginning of this chapter, private entrepreneurs have been, and will continue to be, the primary owners of IU's. The trend toward commercial failures of IU's initiated by private proprietors will probably continue as well. The reasons for failure stem from the lack of knowledge of the *real* resources required to build a successful IU.

Marketing problems and resources have already been touched on in Chapter 2. Design considerations and problems were covered in Chapter 9. There are also operating, planning, and financial problems to be solved. Probably the chief cause of failure will be the lack of realization that very large *technical* resources, especially *software* resources, are required.

For this reason, the private proprietors and organizations with the best chances for long-range IU ownership success are those with access to large systems and software resources. Equipment resources, with the exception of terminals, will not be a determining factor. Therefore, indications are that the following types of organizations, listed at the start of this chapter, will emerge as the most likely owners: private entrepreneurs with access to large systems and software resources, computer service bureaus, large electronic systems companies, and software companies. Communications companies and computer manufacturers could also emerge as likely owners, because they possess these resources, providing the regulatory and marketing strategy situations change.

regulation

Public utilities have been regulated for the protection of public interest and to prevent a natural monopoly from charging exorbitant fees. The same reasoning can be assumed to apply to IU's. In some cases, it no doubt will apply. However, a close examination of the possible monopolistic tendencies, public exploitation, fraud potential, and competitive situations shows that most IU's will be highly competitive indeed and that no requirement for regulation, beyond the normal SEC standards, exists.

Only three types of IU's would seem to require regulation: those handling money and/or financial information, those tending toward complete monopolies, and those providing a true public service. An example of the first type is SAVE. Financial regulation seems essential for SAVE, either at the local level by banking regulatory agencies, or at the national level by the Comptroller of the Currency, the Federal Reserve Board, or the SEC.

An example of the second type is the ticketing service, which has a tendency to become a monopoly. In that case, a certain amount of built-in regulation already exists because of the familiar ticket price structures that the public is used to paying. No ticketing agent can afford to pay, and the IU cannot charge, more than a certain "percentage of the gate," so to speak. In fact, the ticketing service itself, as was mentioned, eliminates or reduces public gouging in the form of scalping or "ice." It will be difficult to determine just what agency could or should regulate the national ticketing service. The same thing will be true of any national IU with monopolistic tendencies. The antitrust section of the Justice Department is surely concerned, but it has not traditionally been a regulating agency.

The current FCC hearings have invited all interested organizations to comment on IU's, but surely the FCC is *not* the proper agency to regulate information utilities. Communications, as can be seen from the descriptions and types of IU's, are only an incidental part of the overall service.

Communications regulation involves a completely different set of problems than IU regulation. Certainly, the FCC should and will continue to regulate the *communications services* that make it possible for IU's to operate.

Perhaps, out of the FCC hearings will come an understanding of the need for, as well as the lack of need for, regulation of IU's. And perhaps from that new understanding on the part of the federal government, as well as other participants, will emerge a new agency. This new agency might be called the Federal Information Utilities Agency, and it might be given jurisdiction over any IU's where regulation is required.

As for the third type of IU, one providing a true public service, in the public utility sense of the word, none would appear to exist now or to be on the horizon, although a hospital IU where public safety is involved may come close.

The large majority of IU's created in the 1960's have not been regulated and probably never will be. The general purpose problem solving types are so highly competitive that the subscriber can really take his pick. Service charges are very low, and in any given local community several choices are available. In fact, competition has forced, and will continue to force, mergers and acquisitions, or dropouts.

The industry oriented IU's have not been regulated, although many are nonprofit organizations. The exceptions are the savings institution IU's, in which the handling of money is involved. These IU's are regulated by local banking groups, usually state agencies.

The stock brokerage IU's are not regulated, although the information they supply to subscribers must be approved by the various stock exchanges and the SEC, which controls the exchanges' operations.

Hospital, educational and teaching, railroad, airline, insurance, publishing, etc., IU's will require policing by their own industries but not regulation. One other IU possibly requiring national regulation will be the public survey and polling service. The FCC or the SEC could very well decide to regulate automated public polling services for the same reasons that manually taken polls have come under scrutiny. However, congressional action would be required in this case.

Criminal intelligence, post office, and governmental information retrieval IU's are, by nature, already under state or federal control. However, the public requires some protection in these cases as well. More will be said on this subject in the next chapter.

auditing

The problem of insuring accuracy, nonfraudulent activity, and proper accounting techniques for an IU is as unique as the design considerations. Auditing procedures have had to undergo basic changes just to keep pace with batch processing computer systems. Then OLRT introduced an entirely new set of problems because of the disappearance of nearly all visible records. Finally, the IU multiplies the OLRT problems by another factor, because large numbers of subscribing organizations as well as the IU organization itself must be audited.

One simplifying proposed solution is to have an audit performed periodically of the IU organization by an outside firm, which, by extension, audits all of the subscribers' records as well. Since subscriber records, probably including money balances, are all in the same physical location and yet all intermixed in sometimes completely untraceable (except by the superlanguage memory) locations, it is obvious that special auditing techniques must be developed.

To sum up, the individual or organization planning to start an IU must take a certain amount of risk with regard to potential regulation, potential competition, or public protection. The situation is so complex that things will probably not settle down for many years.

federal government position

The federal government has taken an active interest in IU's since the mid-1960's. Among the agencies that have conducted studies or held hearings or played an active role in creating IU's are:

1. *Advanced Research Projects Agency of the Department of Defense.* ARPA, as mentioned in Chapter 3, sponsored many of the early developments in general purpose problem solving IU's.

2. *The National Commission on Technology, Automation, and Economic Progress.* This commission, formed by President Johnson in 1964, assigned Professor Merrill M. Flood, then on leave of absence from the University of Michigan and working at Project MAC at MIT, to head a study of information utilities. Professor Flood wrote a lengthy report, portions of which were incorporated into the report of the commission.[2]

3. *Federal Communications Commission.* The series of hearings being held by the FCC have been referred to frequently in prior chapters. Actually, the FCC hearings are much broader than just the communications aspects of IU's and broader than the FCC's normal scope of interests and activities. Over a two-year period, the hearings have resulted in the first phase, during which many organizations filed statements of interest and position. Among these were all computer companies (through BEMA), all communications companies, several IU's, many service bureaus, and many trade associations. As already predicted earlier, the likely outcome of the hearings will be a brand-new government agency, probably at department level, to regulate those IU's and other computer based systems requiring regulation. The FCC is likely to continue to regulate only the communications services supplied to all IU owners by common carriers.

4. *Antitrust Division of the Justice Department.* This department is interested in preventing, but not necessarily regulating, the monopolistic tendencies in IU's that would be detrimental to public interest. The division has taken and continues to take an active interest in the FCC hearings. While the Justice Department has not taken a public position on any aspect and has not filed a statement, nevertheless it has asked to attend all hearings and to be given copies of all statements filed by any other organizations.

5. *Federal Reserve Board and Federal Reserve System.* The

2. National Commission on Technology, Automation, and Economic Progress, *Final Report to the President and Congress* (Washington, D.C.: Government Printing Office, 1966).

board of governors of the Federal Reserve System have taken an active interest and, in the case of Governor Mitchell, a positive position with regard to SAVE. The Federal Reserve System sponsored a nationwide study by Stanford Research Institute on the checkless society and its impact on the Federal Reserve System as well as on the national economy.[3] The impact was shown to be enormous; on the order of 8 billion dollars per year in national savings can result from the implementation of SAVE. The Federal Reserve then announced its intention of establishing its own IU centers at various Federal Reserve banking locations.

6. *Comptroller of the Currency.* James Saxon, when Comptroller of the Currency, was vitally interested in SAVE and stated that his office would do everything possible to make it legal for banks to become owners and operators of SAVE.[4] Certain changes in banking regulations will be necessary for this situation to come about.

7. *National Science Foundation.* This government agency has sponsored much research in the field of IU's. One example is the creation of a national retrieval IU for chemical compounds. NSF financed a study of the feasibility of creating such an IU and is backing the chemical societies and organizations in starting its formation.

8. *Department of Commerce.* The Bureau of Standards under the Department of Commerce has been responsible for much research in the design and standardization of IU technology.

9. *United States of America Standards Institute (USASI).* While not a federal agency, this quasi-governmental organization is responsible for establishing technical standards, many of which will be useful in IU's. Examples are personal and organizational identification standards, data communications standards, and computer-to-computer compatibility.

10. *Department of Defense.* DOD has sponsored and is planning to sponsor many national IU's. The department itself will also own and operate several information utilities. Perhaps the most important of these is to be a national technical document retrieval IU. DOD agencies, such as the Office of Naval Research, Air

3. Bonner Cox, *Research Report on Electronic Check Transfers to Federal Reserve Board* (Menlo Park, California: Stanford Research Institute, 1966).
4. Author's interview with James Saxon, 1966.

Force Research and Development, and the Office of the Secretary of Defense for Information, also sponsor much IU research.

11. *Congress.* When and if new laws are passed to regulate IU's or to eliminate the invasion of privacy, Congress will of course be involved. It is to be hoped that congressional knowledge and interest in IU's will increase beyond the level of the Gallagher and Long committees.

part iv   today and tomorrow

The last part of the book ties together all the other parts in order to demonstrate the probable validity of the opening prediction. It is shown that the emergence of information utilities, and the rapid growth forecasted for them in the latter half of the twentieth century, will have a tremendous impact on the individual and on society.

The new information revolution of man–computer teamwork predicted at the beginning of the book is brought into focus through specific examples and general discussion of the impact of the information utility on individuals, on business, on education, on government, on law, and on society.

11 *impact on individuals, and sociological implications*

The impact on individuals of IU developments and what they can lead to will be not only startling but nearly unbelievable in today's world. By the year 2000, our grandchildren will be telling their children about the days in the 1960's when people used to get along without thinking aids. This is somewhat like having our grandparents telling us about the good old days when people somehow survived without automobiles, television, telephones, or hearing aids.

mental processes

The concept that a man–computer partnership, like a man–hearing aid partnership, can increase man's intellectual capabilities as well as simplify his everyday problems is difficult to grasp today. Yet many of our children are already learning to live with and make use of this partnership in the classroom and in special study booths. Even today, engineers, scientists, and operations researchers are solving problems and designing complex structures in a new intellectual way.

It is this impact on the way the mind works that is truly significant. Imagine multiplying your instantaneous memory capacity by a factor of ten almost overnight. Not even the famous Roth memory course could do that. Yet, that is exactly what will happen as a result of humans using the new tools that IU's can provide. Memory, reasoning, logical capability, decision making, planning, self-analysis, and many other mental effects will result from the new partnership.

There will be a double effect taking place. First, the man–IU partnership will be able to accomplish more than the sum of their individual accomplishments. This is the synergistic effect. Second, man's own mental capabilities, especially memory, will increase even when the partnership is not operating.

Taking memory increase as an example, the reasons for both effects taking place can be seen if it is assumed that the service described as PDS is available. First, the interaction between PDS and the individual enables the partnership to find anything in the memory of either, starting with only a vague hint as to the item sought. Each reinforces the other as the individual browses through the files and as PDS helps make all of the associations among data elements.

As the individual finally locates the item sought, his immediate memory is filled with a series of visual patterns from the screen of his CRT. Visual patterns are stronger, in terms of memory reinforcement, than any other of the five senses. These patterns form a trail, in effect, that reminds the individual, not only about the item sought, but the relationships that caused him to find it. This characteristic is sometimes referred to as associative memory. A person tries to recall a name, and associates it with a face, or physical appearance, or the person's home town, or his age, or sex, or his old maiden aunt, or the company he worked for, or the time and place they met years ago, or any one or more of a thousand other things. The Roth memory course forces a person to associate a name and face with something else, like another similar name. The trick works if the association is reinforced often enough.

When PDS comes into extensive use, an individual's visual reinforcements of the *key* associations he needs will occur over and over again. Thus, his memory for those things that are currently active and most needed should vastly improve.

Another cumulative impact on man's intellect can be anticipated for those individuals who begin using educational and teaching services in their formative years. This effect can seem, at first, somewhat like giving a person a crutch and then worrying about whether he will fall when it is taken away. However, on a long-range basis, the same result can be expected that is predictable with PDS influencing the memory on a short-range basis. An individual who learns and studies from the ages of 6 through 21, using IU terminals in the classroom, the library, study booths, and at home, is bound to feel a permanent impact on his intellectual capacity. In addition, he will, of course, continue to use terminals and IU services in his office, his home, his laboratory, and in other places for the rest of his life.

activity impact

The reader has already begun to see for himself the impact of IU's on his various personal activities. Here is a list of changes in his life and the IU's that will bring them about.

1. Any individual will be able to:
   a. Wait a shorter time at the window of his savings bank. (Savings account service)
   b. Obtain better and faster information from his stock-broker over the phone, or by direct use of a terminal in his broker's customer room. (Stock quotation service)
   c. Make all of his travel reservations in *one phone call* to his travel agent, with guaranteed confirmations on airlines, hotels, car rental, etc. in several cities before hanging up. (Travel service)
   d. Be assured that his credit is checked correctly when opening a new charge account and that the credit standing moves rapidly with him to a new community. (National credit service)
   e. Pay for everything with one card, receive free overdraft money injections, run his financial affairs better, and eliminate bill paying. (SAVE)
   f. Study and learn more rapidly, at his own pace, and with a new mental capability. (Educational IU)
   g. Make a hotel reservation anywhere in any hotel with one local call. (Hotel reservation service)
   h. Be assured of all interairline reservations when travelling on several airlines in one trip. (Interairline reservation service)
   i. Purchase a ticket on the spot for any reserved seat event anywhere. (Ticketing service)
   j. File his income tax return with accuracy and speed

through the screen of a CRT terminal, with all deductions and computations handled and checked automatically. (Tax service)

k. Find a new job that most closely matches his capabilities anywhere in the country, and test his own "job market value" without revealing his identity. (Career information)

l. Create his own set of files and memory aids. (PDS)

2. If he is a lawyer, he will be able to:
   a. Find legal citations rapidly and thoroughly. (Legal citation service)
   b. Bill his clients more efficiently and accurately. (Professional billing service)
   c. Handle all of his bookkeeping. (General purpose)
   d. Do his clients' tax returns, using a CRT. (Tax service)
   e. Set up his own set of personal office files. (PDS)

3. If he is a doctor, he will be able to:
   a. Analyze a patient's condition and treatment faster and more accurately. (Hospital-medical service)
   b. Perform laboratory tests faster and better and monitor a critical patient's condition better. (Hospital service)
   c. Bill his patients more accurately and efficiently. (Professional billing)

4. If she is a secretary, she will be able to:
   a. Receive assistance in typing and editing. (Typing and editing service)
   b. Handle her bosses' travel arrangements more assuredly and efficiently. (Travel, airline, hotel, and ticket services)
   c. Find things in the file better. (PDS)
   d. Help her boss remember. (PDS)

The housewife and the executive, the engineer, the scientist, and the graphical designer have already been discussed.

Perhaps the most difficult impact to evaluate as far as individuals are concerned is the change in communication mode or relationship to other individuals and to organizations. Some of this potential impact has already been discussed in Chapter 6.

There would seem to be little question that changes will take place. Office organizational structures, and even physical arrangements will change. Some optimists predict the eventual elimination of all paper in the office.[1] When two people in different locations can look at their own screens, see the same thing, then talk to each other by phone while changing the displays on their screens, the conclusion must be reached that communications between individuals will change.

big brother — 1984

The immediate reaction by some people to all of these ideas is fear. It is usually expressed as indignation about machines taking over everything, or the invasion of privacy. Nevertheless, it is really fear: fear of becoming less intelligent compared to the average, or fear of something mysterious and incomprehensible.

Some fears *are* justified. Congressional committees really are concerned about the invasion of privacy of individuals that might occur or be made easier by the creation of "National Data Centers" covering all people. In the late 1960's, Congressman Cornelius Gallagher of New Jersey, Senator Edward Long of Missouri, and Vance Packard in his various publications expressed major concerns over the possibility that George Orwell's 1984 was creeping up on the American public. It was feared that a national credit information utility, which began to take shape in 1966, and might eventually become SAVE, would invade the financial privacy of every citizen.

The strange anomaly of the invasion of privacy situation is that *it can only be prevented by a "National IU for Individuals."*

What most people, including Vance Packard and Congressmen Gallagher and Long, did not know was that their own privacy was, and still is, being invaded every day in countless ways. If they had had the intestinal courage re-

1. Joe Spiegel, "The Electronic Executive," in the Proceedings of the Spring Joint Computer Conference, Boston, Mass., April 27, 1966.

quired, credit managers and credit bureau operators could have told Mr. Gallagher the truth about what goes on all of the time. So could the FBI, state and local police, private detectives, and many lawyers, not to mention wiretapping and bugging experts and the telephone companies. In late 1968, a congressional investigation of credit bureaus began to discover *some*, but only a small fraction, of this dirty linen. The trouble is that all of the invasion of privacy that has been occurring for years is secret, or supposedly secret. The only people not "in on the secret" are Mr. and Mrs. Average Citizen.

A visit to any retail credit bureau, bank credit bureau, or legal information bureau on any day of the week can be most revealing (provided the manager does not know about the visit). First of all, information in *your* file contains every negative thing that ever happened to you, going back to the beginning of your credit life. The data is never updated, corrected, or weeded out. It includes not just credit data, such as failures to make installment payments on time, but also any legal actions taken against you, divorce or offspring problem reports, newspaper clippings, private detective investigations, FBI or police reports including interviews with gossipy biased neighbors, etc.

There are very bad things about this invasion of privacy. First, and foremost, *you* do not even know the file exists, much less know what is in it. Second, even if you did know it existed, you would not be permitted to look at it unless you happen to be a credit bureau subscriber. Then, you can buy a report about yourself or anyone else, for that matter, for about $1.50. However, do not rush out to buy one as soon as you read this. Mr. and Mrs. John Q. Public are not eligible to become credit bureau subscribers. The report on you that others can buy summarizes the information in the file in a simple good, bad, average type of credit code. Who did the summarizing? Not an unbiased impersonal computer? Oh no! It was a human being in the credit bureau, or in the one covering you in the community from which you just moved. He is personal and biased. He is bound to be.

The subscribers can have the entire file on you for somewhat more money. Legislation was being suggested by a congressional committee in late 1968 that would make it possible for you to buy a copy of your own file.

But the third bad thing is that *you* can do nothing about changing the contents of your own file even if you could get a look at it. You see, it does not belong to you; it belongs to the credit bureau.

The fourth bad thing is that the information in your file is old, inaccurate, obsolete, and incomplete with no interpretation or explanations. You are as bad now as you ever were at your worst. One committee witness, in December 1968, said that he bought an airplane on the credit standing of his company, while his wife could not even make a small purchase in a store because of an event that took place in their personal life years ago. The whole point here is that by their very nature, the credit and legal information bureau businesses are interested mainly in negative data. Nothing good or positive ever comes through or finds its way into your file, and if it does it is overwhelmed by negative information.

What is that you say? I have never done anything wrong and I have always paid my bills on time. OK, good for you, if it is true. But is it? What about that time around twelve years ago when you switched jobs and had to hold up on the refrigerator payment for a month or two? And what about that little argument you had with the real estate agent over a property line. You won, but it resulted in a threatened lawsuit. Both will be in your record even if they did not make the papers, and the record will not show why you were late or that you won the argument without going to court.

The fifth bad aspect about this invasion of privacy is that any subscriber or legal agency can look at your record, and *you do not know it*. Who are the subscribers to the credit bureau? Practically everyone but you. They include all other credit bureaus for bankers, retailers, insurance companies, credit card companies, plus *any* organization to which you might apply for credit.

Worse yet, during that secret visit to the bureau, you might see FBI agents, Secret Service agents, CIA agents, state policemen, city detectives, and maybe a private eye or two, all looking at records. Some of them spend a lot of time there, and any one of them could be examining your inaccurate, obsolete record without your knowledge. For what purpose? Perhaps a check on security clearance, perhaps as a result of a false tip someone gave out, or perhaps because your wife or boss paid a detective to do some checking.

The retail credit bureaus, the bank credit bureaus, and the legal information bureaus are only the beginning. All over the United States, there are files on you that you do not know about, cannot look at, and cannot change no matter how inaccurate or obsolete they are. Some examples: at FBI headquarters, CIA headquarters, Social Security Administration, Internal Revenue Service, Department of Labor, Veterans Administration, your insurance company, motor vehicle bureau, your credit card companies, individual retailers and banks, hospitals, trade associations, professional societies, Blue Cross . . . The list goes on and on.

Some of these files are in better shape than those at the credit bureau. Some have a lot less information in them. It is unlikely that any two of them will agree on any collection of data about you. Their uses are multifarious. Take for example, the FBI and CIA files on you. If you have ever been fingerprinted, and who has not, you are in the FBI files. You are also possibly in certain state police files.

All of this secret filing has been going on for years. It constitutes invasion of privacy to the nth degree, and none of what has been said so far involves computers. In fact, the introduction of computers helps clean things up a bit, or at least reduces the total amount of data about you. Machine storage just is not conducive to holding a newspaper clipping or a photograph or a gossipy report about you.

the national information utility for individuals

How will a national IU help solve the problem? With a single national record storage capability, coupled with a new law, invasion of privacy can be ended. Here is how it can be done. A law would be passed with the following provisions:

1. There will be one and only one *legal* record on each individual citizen from birth.

2. The citizen or his legal guardians will have the right to examine the record at any time. Periodically, the citizen will be informed of changes made in the record.

3. The citizen will have the right to change (delete, correct, update, add) his own record at any time by legally constituted means.

4. The citizen will be informed either periodically or upon occurrence whenever any person or organization examines his record and will be told the name and purpose of the examiner.

5. All other records pertaining to the citizen will be declared illegal and null and void.

6. Access to each citizen's record will be granted according to an application procedure similar to those in existence in credit bureaus and other record keeping organizations.

Physically, the records need not all be in the same place. The most natural IU network will be one in which there are regional centers, and the citizen's record is stored in the region of his legal residence. It will move whenever he moves. A communications network interconnecting all centers will provide for inquiries between regions. As in the case of SAVE, a large majority of the inquiries into records and changes in them will remain within the region.

There can still be other records on the individual and no doubt will be, but they will not be legal records and will have limited use.

The development of the SAVE service almost demands that such a national citizens IU be established. Individual identity probably should and could be established by always using either the Social Security or the new unique birth number, which is now being assigned to everyone born in the United States.

This entire concept will, of course, be very unpopular with habitual criminals. It will also be very unpopular with the FBI, CIA, state and local police, private detectives, and the Secret Service, who would all prefer that their examinations of records be kept secret. Yet, unless the public demands it, Big Brother will *continue* to watch you.

are machines taking over

The other type of fear, that of life becoming too mechanical, too dominated by machines and numbers, is only partially legitimate. Certainly, machines are not going to take over the world. However, it is possible for an unscrupulous individual or organization to *use* machines or IU's to take advantage of the public. Thus, we have the need for regulation.

The reason machines are not taking over is that they are nothing more than tools for human use. The services provided by IU's are completely under the control of men and, in most cases, are optional as far as usage is concerned. The world of 2000 will have just as many, and probably more, creative, artistic individuals who will never go near many IU services. However, their memory capacities may not be as great, on the average, as subscribers to PDS or educational IU's. The initial resistance to many IU services will disappear very rapidly and the fears will go away when their advantages become obvious from watching those who use them.

12 *impact on business, and economic considerations*

business impact

Information utilities will have nearly as great an impact on the world of business as they will on individuals. Previous chapters have illustrated how the impact on specific industries will be caused by utilities designed for those industries. Examples described were airlines, savings institutions, stock brokerage firms, travel agencies, credit bureaus, hospital and medical organizations, hotels, educational institutions, and local merchants.

The most important effect that these industry oriented information utilities will have is on the small company which can take advantage of data processing and information storage facilities formerly available only to their large competitors.

A second impact will be the intercommunication made possible by the IU among all companies in the industry. The total business of the industry will be enhanced. Examples are in airlines, stock brokerage, travel, credit, and hotels.

A third type of business impact will be the multi-industry or organizational intercommunication situation represented by SAVE, the ticketing service, and the tax service.

A fourth kind of impact will be the effects that will be felt in the business office and the gradual disappearance of paper as a means of recording and communicating information. The typing and editing service, personal data services, data retrieval services, document retrieval services, career and employment information service, travel service, ticketing service, airline and hotel reservations, and SAVE all will have an impact on office procedures.

the large company

An example of the effect on a large company can best be given by describing what things could be like in the year

2000. All of the top management levels in the company are using CRT terminals and so are the secretaries. The secretaries use a typing and editing service for most of their work. They can communicate with their bosses via the CRT terminals. The executives and both line and staff people are using the PDS service as individuals and in groups as large as a department.

The secretaries of the executives who do a lot of traveling can have their terminals connected directly to the national travel service. Other people in the company can go to or call up special travel and ticket desks in each major plant and office location. These desks are equipped with both ticket and travel reservation service terminals.

The company also subscribes to the national tax service, with terminals located in the tax departments to permit higher level employees to file their own tax returns. The tax departments also file the corporate return on the central terminal.

Some of the top executives and the corporate investment group in the treasurer's office subscribe to one of the national stock market services. They use special terminals for this service.

The management sciences group in the engineering department and scientific and engineering personnel in the research laboratories, are using several different kinds of terminals to dial up several different general purpose problem solving and graphical design utility services. In addition, the technical libraries in several different company locations subscribe to document retrieval and library catalog services. The accounting department uses SAVE for all payroll transfers, bill payments, and corporate financial planning and budgeting. The marketing division subscribes to a merchandising and advertising service, a public survey service, and a marketing research service. The personnel department uses several terminals for employee searching provided by the national employment utility service. Finally, the legal department subscribes to a legal citation service and a labor negotiating service.

The economics of signing up for all of these services are simple. Two basic cases occur that favor outside utilities for performing certain services rather than have them performed inside the company's own system. The first is the situation in which the service, by its nature, can only be provided by a utility. The second is the case of economy of scale, in which the large utility and the large number of subscribers bring down the cost per subscriber far below that of an inside system.

the small company

In the case of a small company, all or most of the services mentioned for the large company will be good possibilities. Depending on whether the small company's industry is comparable to the airline or savings institution industries, the entire range of information processing functions may be provided by an industry utility.

In any event, it is likely that a general purpose data processing utility will provide the small company's accounting oriented functions from inventory control and customer billing through general ledger and management reports. Keydata Corporation actually started off with this concept for small distributing companies in the mid-1960's.

economic considerations

From the early days of information utilities, a great deal of controversy has swirled around the general question of the cost justification or economics of buying outside utility services. The pro-utility people contend that economies of scale are always bound to win out. The cons say that costs of software and other hidden costs in a really large-scale utility will more than eat up any savings brought about by spreading costs over a large number of users.

This argument, which was still raging in the late 1960's, concerned primarily the time sharing or general purpose problem solving utility. Unfortunately for the pros, the software costs for this type of utility, in the early versions, were very high. The economies of scale were not felt as rapidly as the forecasts would have had subscribers believe. The introduction of new hardware, such as SAFORS (see Chapter 9), might have changed the economics of the situation, but this type of development had not begun by the end of the 1960's.

However, the proliferation of information utility services by 1969 indicated that either the economic difficulties had been solved or else had been highly overemphasized by the cons. The explanation is probably a combination of both. The cons overlooked the fact that many IU's do not have all of the software problems that a general purpose type has. The savings institution IU, for example, has such a small amount of variation from one subscriber's requirements to another's that its software is nearly the same as all of the self-contained systems and all other IU's in the savings industry. So an economy of scale in a number of nearly identical software packages for the same type of IU is a factor to be considered.

Nevertheless, the major factor in causing the economics of an IU to be overlooked is the unique and proprietary nature of the service. If we use the ticket reservation service as an example, the subscriber cannot really evaluate it on a cost justification basis any more than he can justify his own telephone. The service is unique. Without it the subscriber cannot meet competition. He cannot be concerned with its cost as long as it is not completely unreasonable.

The cost justification or cost displacement ground rules that tended to govern the batch processing systems acquisition decisions in the 1950's and 1960's just do not apply to IU services. PDS, for example, must be measured in completely different terms than a payroll or accounts receivable system. There will probably be no displaceable costs at all in an executive level PDS service. What has to be evaluated is the saving of time of the executive or the overall value to the organization of better decisions brought about by PDS by the top level executives.

inside versus outside IU service

Another economic comparison governing the decision to purchase outside IU services is the one referred to earlier, of the cost of an outside IU service versus the cost of the same function as part of an internal system. This comparison has been made most frequently for engineering problem solving (time sharing) services.

The total number of internal subscribers must be divided into the total incremental costs of adding the time sharing capabilities to the internal system. If an organization has a very large number of users, a commercially available internal time sharing system can compare favorably with an external IU service.[1] The incremental costs to add time sharing capabilities to an existing internal system can be difficult to compute and can be very high. Even an existing internal OLRT system will probably not have the proper software characteristics to permit the addition of time sharing facilities.

The large majority of time sharing terminals are connected to information utilities rather than internal systems, because a very small percentage of the engineers, operations researchers, scientists, and mathematicians who would like to have their own terminals are in organizations (excluding universities) large enough to justify their own time sharing systems.

component costs

The economics of information utility services will change drastically as the costs of terminals are reduced. Terminal cost is a very high percentage of the lowest possible cost of

1. Time sharing systems are being sold to large organizations by Scientific Data Systems, General Electric, IBM, RCA, Univac, Digital Equipment Corporation, Control Data Corporation, and Hewlett Packard.

IU service for a single subscriber. It represents the irreducible minimum cost per subscriber. New developments in the late 1960's foreshadow a drastic reduction in terminal costs in the 1970's.

Terminal costs (excluding the telephone) had been in the $2,000 to $10,000 range, with rentals of $50 to $500 per month. A CRT terminal carried a minimum cost of $5,000 with a rental of $125 a month. A large percentage of the cost of a CRT terminal is in the electronic circuitry, or so-called logic. By drastically reducing the costs of this portion of the terminals, the service can achieve a substantial overall reduction.

The new developments just referred to had been achieved in 1968 by two companies, Viatron Corporation of Burlington, Massachusetts, and Computer Communications, Inc., of Inglewood, California. CCI separated the problems of designing the cathode ray tube device itself from designing the rest of the terminal. They started with a standard commercial television set and designed electronic circuits to move the beam of the set in the desired visual patterns. As a result of using this approach, they were able to reduce the terminal cost by nearly 2 to 1 compared to the next lowest cost CRT terminal. The 1968 selling price for a CCI terminal was in the $4000-$5000 range. A much larger percentage of the CRT terminal cost, in the case of CCI, is invested in the electronic circuitry.

Viatron attacked the cost of the electronics by introducing large-scale integration (LSI) techniques into terminal design. LSI had, prior to the Viatron development, been used exclusively for central computer circuitry. LSI involves a new crystalline growth concept in which the entire circuitry of the terminal is manufactured all at once by a heating process. Assembly operations and costs are reduced nearly to zero. LSI was developed originally for military electronic devices under government financing. The Viatron costs were still being reduced by early 1969. An off-line CRT terminal had been announced to rent for under $40 per month, a reduction of better than 2 to 1 over competition.

If these two developments are combined, as they no doubt will be by many suppliers in the early 1970's, costs for CRT type general purpose terminals should be further reduced. Selling prices of well under $1000, and rentals in the $10 to $25 per month range, can be anticipated.

As far as other cost components are concerned, reductions can be expected in central IU hardware and software and in data communications. However, the magnitude of these reductions will not be as great as the terminal cost reduction. Changes in IU central facility system design, such as SAFORS, may produce a 20 to 30 per cent reduction. Changes in FCC regulatory arrangements and changes resulting from the hearings on IU's should produce communications cost savings of the same order.

The net result of all component cost reductions should produce an overall 2 to 1 potential reduction in IU service charges within the next few years. By the year 2000, costs will have been reduced and the market will have become large enough that the housewife's PDS service should cost no more than twice her current telephone bill.

appendixes and index

tables

Table 2-2   *Examples of information utilities*

type	current examples (1968)
1. Savings account processing	Savings & Loan Bank of N. Y.; NCR; Burroughs; North Federal S & L Ass'n., Chicago; Union Dime; Champion Service Corp., Cleveland; Bank of St. Louis; Harris Trust, Chicago
2. Stock brokerage information	Stockmaster, Quotron, Telequote, Aut-Ex, Standard & Poor's, Compustat, NASDAQ
3. Travel service	Telemax, General Data Corp., SAFIR
4. Professional billing	Medac, several banks
5. Engineering problem solving	MIT's MAC and ICES, Dartmouth–GE, IBM's Quiktran, GE–Information Processing Business, Ford's Technical Computing Center, Bell Labs., Carnegie Inst. of Tech., Ohio State Univ., Perkin Elmer Corp., Rand Corp., TRW Systems Group, CEIR, Stanford Univ., System Development Corp., Computer Sciences Corp., Applied Logic Corp., Tyme Share Ass'n., Univ. of Calif. at Santa Barbara, Com-Share, Inc., Service Bureau Corp., Bolt Beranek & Newman's Telecomp
6. Graphical design	General Motors–IBM, DAC 1, Itek, Philco's Graphden, MIT's Sketchpad, Rand Corp.'s GRAIL, DEC's Graphpad
7. Document retrieval	Law societies, Federal Government agencies, Library of Congress, MIT's Project Intrex, IBM-1350 Photo Image Retrieval
8. Data retrieval	Ultronics' Recallit, PDS
9. General purpose	Keydata Corp., GE, Service Bureau Corp., Statistical Tabulating Corp.'s Dial-O-Mat, Western Union
10. Credit information	Credit Data Corp., Telecredit, Pacific NW Credit Bureaus, ACB of A
11. Financial exchange — SAVE	Payment Systems, Inc., Bank of Delaware
12. Hospital and medical	Dartmouth College–Mary Hitchcock Hospital; GE–Medinet–Mass. General; Minn. Blue Cross; Kettering Memorial,

	Dayton; Children's Hospital Medical Center, Boston; Sara Mayo–Tulane Univ.; Indianapolis Hospital Development Ass'n.
13. Educational and teaching	Florida Atlantic Univ., North Carolina Center, Bureau of Naval Personnel, State of Illinois, Dist. of Philadelphia, State Univ. of N. Y. at Buffalo, Univ. of Penn., West Point, Purdue, Univ. of Washington, Univ. of New Mexico, Univ. of Utah, Dartmouth, Rensselaer Poly. Institute, UCLA Western Data Center, Boston high schools–Bolt Beranek & Newman, Univ. of Calif. at Santa Barbara
14. Hotel reservations	General Data Corporation
15. Interairline reservations	ATARS (Informatics — Hayden Stone), CDC's SAFIR
16. Railroad information	Midwestern Bank, Canadian System, Raildata Corp.
17. Publishing	Rocappi, Inc.
18. Radio and TV time brokerage	
19. Retail and distribution	National Association of Wholesalers, GE
20. Insurance	Recording and statistical
21. Merchandising and advertising	Teleprompter, Westinghouse's direct mail
22. Public survey and polling	Teleprompter, Zenith, Roper Public Opinion Research Center
23. Sport and theatre tickets	Teleticket Corporation, Ticket Reservation Systems
24. Tax service	Litton's Datatax, CSC's Computax
25. Labor negotiations	AFL-CIO Industrial Union Dept.
26. Career and employment information	Personnel Information Communication System — Western Union
27. Legal citation service	Legal Research Service, Inc. — Western Union
28. Post office	CDC's Postal Source Data
29. Marketing research	IBM's Industry Information Service Reports, IT & T World Trade Statistics
30. Criminal intelligence	National Crime Information Center
31. Typing and editing service	IBM's Datatext
32. Personal data services	PDS Corporation
33. Library catalogs	Library of Congress — Project MARC
34. Lottery service	New York State (under consideration)

Table 2-3 (next five pages) *Types of services offered to information utility service users. C—currently offered; P—potential market. Note: Data in this table change rapidly. This information was up-to-date in 1967.*

types of user organizations	savings account processing	stock brokerage information	travel service including hotel and airline reservations
manufacturing companies			
1. Automotive			
2. Paper			
3. Steel			
4. Other metals			
5. Electrical			
6. Petroleum			
7. Chemical			
8. Aerospace			
9. Food products			
10. Pharmaceuticals			
distribution industries			
11. Department stores			
12. Specialty chains			
13. Discounters			
14. Variety chains			
15. Mail order			
16. Wholesalers			
17. Dealers			
18. Food chains			
19. Drug chains			
20. Warehouses			
financial concerns			
21. Commercial banks	C	C	
22. Savings institutions	C	P	
23. Finance companies	P		
24. Brokerage firms		C	
others			
25. Investment		C	
26. Construction firms			
27. Insurance companies		P	
28. Real estate firms			
29. Lawyers		P	
30. Doctors			
31. Architects			
32. Engineering firms			
33. State government			
34. Local government			
35. Hospitals and medical			
36. Educational institutions			
37. Travel agents			C
38. Libraries			
39. Credit organizations			
40. Transportation companies			C
41. Hotels and restaurants			C
42. Publishing and printing			
43. Radio, TV and communcation			
44. Advertising agencies			
45. Accounting firms			
46. Students			
47. Consumers	P		P
48. Public utilities			

	professional billing	engineering problem solving	scientific programming and operations research	graphical design
1.		C	C	C
2.		C	C	P
3.		C	C	C
4.		C	C	C
5.		C	C	C
6.		C	C	P
7.		C	C	P
8.		C	C	C
9.			C	P
10.		C	C	P
11.			P	
12.			P	
13.			P	
14.			P	
15.			P	
16.			P	
17.			P	
18.			P	
19.			P	
20.			P	
21.			C	
22.			C	
23.			P	
24.			C	
25.			C	
26.		C	C	C
27.			P	
28.	P			
29.	C			
30.	C			
31.	P	P	C	C
32.	P	C	C	C
33.			P	
34.			P	
35.				P
36.		C	C	C
37.	P			
38.			P	P
39.				
40.		C	C	P
41.				
42.			P	P
43.			P	P
44.	P		P	
45.	P		P	
46.		C	C	C
47.				
48.				

	document retrieval	file storage searching and data retrieval	credit information	save	accounts receivable and billing
1.	P	P		P	P
2.	P	P		P	P
3.	P	P		P	P
4.	P	P		P	C
5.	P	P		P	P
6.	P	P	P	P	P
7.	P	P		P	P
8.	P	P		P	P
9.	P	P		P	P
10.	P	P		P	P
11.		P	P	P	P
12.		P	P	P	P
13.		P	P	P	C
14.		P	P	P	C
15.		P	P	P	P
16.		P	P	P	C
17.		P	P	P	C
18.		P	P	P	P
19.		P	P	P	P
20.		P	P	P	C
21.		P	P	P	
22.		P	P	P	
23.		P	P	P	P
24.		P	P	P	P
25.		P	P	P	P
26.	P	P		P	P
27.	P	P	P	P	P
28.	P	P	P	P	
29.	P	P		P	
30.	P	P		P	
31.	P	P		P	
32.	P	P		P	P
33.	P	P		P	P
34.	P	P		P	P
35.	P	P		P	C
36.	P	P		P	P
37.		P	P	P	P
38.	P	P			
39.		P	P	P	P
40.		P	P	P	C
41.		P	P	P	C
42.	P	P		P	
43.	P	P		P	P
44.		P		P	P
45.	P	P		P	C
46.	P	P			
47.	P		P	P	
48.	P	P	P	P	C

	accounts payable	payroll	inventory control	hospital service and medical diagnostic processing	general accounting
1.	P	P	P		P
2.	P	P	P		P
3.	P	P	P		P
4.	P	P	C		C
5.	P	P	P		P
6.	P	P	P		P
7.	P	P	P		P
8.	P	P	P		P
9.	P	P	P		P
10.	P	P	P		P
11.	P	P	P	P	P
12.	P	P	P		P
13.	P	P	C		C
14.	P	P	C		C
15.	P	P	P		P
16.	P	P	C		C
17.	P	P	C		C
18.	P	P	P		P
19.	P	P	P		P
20.	P	P	C		C
21.	P	P			P
22.	P	P			P
23.	P	P			P
24.	P	P			P
25.	P	P			P
26.	P	P	P		P
27.	P	P			P
28.		P			P
29.					P
30.				C	P
31.					P
32.	P	P	P		P
33.	P	P	P	P	P
34.	P	P	P	P	P
35.	C	C	C		C
36.	P	P	P		P
37.					P
38.			P		
39.		P			P
40.	P	P	C		P
41.	C	C	C		C
42.			P		P
43.	P	P	C		P
44.	P	P			P
45.	P	C	P		C
46.					
47.					
48.	C	C	C		C

	tax services (information and compilation)	teaching and learning services	marketing information survey and input-output	communication services	personnel search information
1.			C	C	C
2.			C	C	C
3.			C	C	C
4.			C	C	C
5.			C	C	C
6.			C	C	C
7.			C	C	C
8.			C	C	C
9.			C	C	C
10.			C	C	C
11.			P	C	C
12.			P	C	C
13.			P	C	C
14.			P	C	C
15.			C	C	C
16.			P	C	C
17.			P	C	C
18.			P	C	C
19.			P	C	C
20.			P	C	C
21.	P		P	P	C
22.			P	P	C
23.			P	C	C
24.			P	C	C
25.	P		P	C	C
26.			P	C	C
27.			P	C	C
28.	P		P		C
29.					C
30.					C
31.		P	P		C
32.		P	P	C	C
33.	P	P		P	C
34.	P	P		P	C
35.				P	C
36.		C			C
37.			P		C
38.		P			C
39.				P	C
40.			C	C	C
41.			C	C	C
42.			P	C	C
43.			C	C	C
44.			C	C	C
45.	C	P	P	P	C
46.		C			C
47.	C		P		C
48.			C	C	C

RESEARCH ORIENTED TIME-SHARING SYSTEMS

ORGANIZATION	COMPUTER(S)	LANGUAGE(S)	TERMINALS	NO. OF USERS	REMARKS
Bolt Beranek and Newman Inc.[1] Cambridge, Massachusetts	PDP-1D	MIDAS, TELCOMP, STRINGCOMP, IRSCOMP	TT-33(90)	64	Medical information and communications system for hospitals. Also used for computational and data management facility.
Bolt Beranek and Newman Inc. Cambridge, Massachusetts	SDS 940	CAL, FORTRAN II, LISP 1.5, ARPAS, NARP, DDT, SNOBOL, TRAC, QED, TECO	TT(16), ST, KM 105 Display	15	User oriented programming languages with access to data management file handling system and with string handling capability.
Campus Computing Network University of California Los Angeles, California	IBM 360/75	FORTRAN IV, LYRIC, WATFOR, COBOL, PL/1, ALGOL, BASIC, RPG, SNOBOL, URSA	IBM 2260(10) CRT(30)	30	System used for research and education. An IBM 360/91 to be installed early in 1969.
C. S. I. R. O. Canberra City, Australia	CDC 3600, PDP-8	CIDER, INTERP, FRED, STATIST, ALGOL, CALC, FORTRAN, COMPASS, SIMSCRIPT	CDC 210(6), 250, TT(5)	12	General purpose scientific computations.
Dartmouth College Kiewit Computation Center Hanover, New Hampshire	GE-635, DATANET-30 (4)	BASIC, ALGOL, FORTRAN	TT-33(30), 35(94), 37	200	Developed under a grant from the National Science Foundation and in cooperation with General Electric Co. System also available for commercial use.
Edinburgh University Edinburgh, Scotland	Elliot 4130	POP-2	TT(20)	8	MULTI-POP-70, based on POP-2 with ALGOL and FORTRAN operational in late 1969.
General Electric Research & Development Center Schenectady, New York	GE-600	BASIC, ALGOL, DOT, FORTRAN, TRAC	TT-30(70), 35(4)	64	Uses include: scientific programming, data acquisition from experiments, system programming development.
IBM Research Thomas J. Watson Res. Ctr. Yorktown Heights, New York	IBM 7010, 1440	COURSEWRITERX	IBM 1050	38	An experimental system for CAI exploration.
Lawrence Radiation Laboratory University of California Livermore, California	PDP-6(2), CDC 7600, 6600(4), 3600, IBM 7030, 7094(2)	FORTRAN, LISP, PL/1, Assembly Language	TT(200), PLT(10), CRT(16)		Use is mostly scientific computation. PDP-6 computers (locally modified) perform central switching and file maintenance.
Lincoln Laboratory — MIT Lexington, Massachusetts	IBM 360/67[2]	FORTRAN IV, SNOBOL, CMS, Assembler	IBM 2741(56), 2250(3)	32	Establishment of a large computational facility for scientific and engineering research.
Lincoln Laboratory — MIT Lexington, Massachusetts	TX-2	MARK V, VITAL, LEAP, CORAL	TY(5), TT(2), CRT(4), PDP-338, RAND TABLET	7	System features fast response time for on-line graphical communication.
Lockheed Georgia Co. Marietta, Georgia	IBM 360/50	FORTRAN IV	IBM 1050(37), 2260(6)	43	System named RAX, developed from earlier 360/40 system, used mostly for engineering.
MIT Dept. of Civil Eng. Cambridge, Massachusetts	IBM 360/67	COGO, STRUDL, ICETRAN, CDL	IBM 2741(5), 1130	15	System named ICES. Uses include Engineering, Science, Management.
MIT Dept. of Electrical Eng. Cambridge, Massachusetts	PDP-1	ASSEMBLER, LISP, MAD, CALCULATOR, EDITOR	TY(5)	5	Experimental time-sharing system for student use in thesis and research projects.
Northern Electric Co., Ltd. Ottawa, Ontario, Canada	CDC 3300(2)	FORTRAN, PL/1, COBOL, COMPASS	TT(20), TWX(10), CDC 8130(3)	22	Scientific and business use.

Institution	Computer	Languages	Consoles	No.	Description
Ohio State University Columbus, Ohio	IBM 360/50	PL/1	IBM 2741(20), 2260(8)	15	Uses include lens design, circuit analysis, computer-aided design, scientific, engineering and research.
Perkin Elmer Corporation Norwalk, Connecticut	SDS 9300, 930	FORTRAN IV, DDT, META-Symbol, SLIP, SPEED	TT-33, 35, IBM 2741	15	
Project MAC-MIT Artificial Intelligence Group Cambridge, Massachusetts	PDP-6, PDP-10	TECO, MIDAS, LISP STRING, TJ6, DDT	TT-33, 35, 37, GE-760, CRT	13	Software development includes the Project MAC Hand-Eye Manipulator system. I/O devices include 2 vidisectors and 2 mechanical manipulators.
Project MAC-MIT Cambridge, Massachusetts	GE-645	ALGOL, FORTRAN IV, PL/1, MAD, SNOBOL	IBM 2741, CRT, TT-37	50	Multics System; limited operation by Fall of 1968. Prototype System by Spring of 1969.
Purdue University Computer Science Department Lafayette, Indiana	IBM 7094	FORTRAN IV, Line Editing	TT-33(8), IBM 1052	20	7094-CDC 6500 Coupled System is now under development.
RAND Corporation Santa Monica, California	PDP-6	JOSS II	JOSS Consoles(32) TT-33, 35(16)	48	Provision for Inter-Console communication, useful for the simulation of games.
TRW Systems Group Redondo Beach, California	Bunker-Ramo 340	Culler-Fried	Consoles(4)[3] BBN Console(2)	4	On-line system for manipulation, specification and execution of mathematical and symbolic operations with graphical output.
United States Military Academy West Point, New York	GE-225(3)	CADETRAN, CO-GO, FISCAL, VFAP, B.P.	TT-35(25), CRT	27	Remote Time-Sharing undergraduate instructional support such as CAI.
University of California Project GENIE Berkeley, California	SDS-930	LISP, SNOBOL, CAL, DDT, QED, NARP, QSPL	TT-33(4), 35(12), CRT(2)	16	Features hardware address mapping. The SDS 940 system is based on the results of this ARPA sponsored project.
University of California Irvine, California	IBM 360/50	ISIS, CAL	IBM 2741(38), 2260(6)	35	Uses include instruction, administration and research.
University of Massachusetts Amherst, Massachusetts	CDC 3600, PDP-8	BASIC, COGO, SMALL, SYNFUL, LSD, TUDOR, FORTRAN IV	TT-33, 35	64	Uses include education and varied research programs in diverse fields.
University of Michigan Ann Arbor, Michigan	IBM-360/67	FORTRAN IV, PL/1, SNOBOL, GPSS, MAD, SDS, WATFOR, PIL, UMIST	TT-33, 35(200), IBM 2741(5), 1050(5), 2250, 2780	100	Remote terminals include a PDP-8, PDP-9, DEC 338 and an IBM 1130.
University of Pennsylvania Philadelphia, Pennsylvania	IBM 7040, PDP-8	MAP, FORTRAN, LG, COBOL, ALGOL, LISP, IPL-V, MAD, SNOBOL, WATFOR, SPRINT, MULTILANG	TT-33(4), CRT(3)	6	Future plans include development of motion pictures by computer and a system using an IBM 360/65.
University of Pittsburgh Computer Center Pittsburgh, Pennsylvania	IBM 360/50	FORTRAN IV, PIL, PL/1, PENELOPE, ASSEMBLER, Context Editor	TT-33, 35, IBM 1050(4), 2741(40), Friden 7100, Datel Thirty 21, CRT(3)	34	General University research and education. Development of On-line Linc-8 for medical research.

NOTES
1. Developed with the Massachusetts General Hospital under contract from the National Institutes of Health.
2. System as described utilizes 1/2 of the full duplex 360/67.
3. Each console consists of two keyboards and a storage tube display.

Table 3-1 (this page and facing page) Research oriented time sharing systems. (Reproduced by permission of Computer Research Corporation, Newton, Mass.)

Table 3-2 (next four pages) Commercial time sharing systems. (Reproduced
by permission of Computer Research Corporation, Newton, Massachusetts)

COMMERCIAL TIME-SHARING SYSTEMS

ORGANIZATION	COMPUTER	LANGUAGES	TERMINALS	NO. OF USERS
Allen-Babcock Computing, Inc. Palo Alto, California	IBM 360/50	PL/1 (on-line subset)	IBM 2741, 1050 TT-33, 35, 37 Friden 7100 Datel Thirty 21	90
Applied Logic Corp. Princeton, New Jersey	DEC PDP-6, PDP-10	FORTRAN IV, DDT, AIDE, BASIC, LISP, MACRO-10, SNOBOL-6 Compact COBOL	TT-33, 35, 37 CRT, PLT IBM 2741	40
Bolt Beranek and Newman Inc. Cambridge, Massachusetts	PDP-10 PDP-7(3)	TELCOMP-10, LISP, FORTRAN IV, MACRO, SNOBOL	TT-33, 35	32
CDC-CEIR Washington, D.C.	GE-235, 420	BASIC, ALGOL, FORTRAN II, IV	TT-33, 35 Friden 7100	40
Call-A-Computer Raleigh, North Carolina	GE-265	ALGOL, BASIC, BIICAC, FORTRAN II, FORCAC, EDIT	TT-33, 35 PLT, CRT	40
Computer Network Corp. Washington, D.C.	B-5500	FORTRAN IV, ALGOL, BASIC, COBOL	TT-33, 35, CRT	32
Computer Sharing, Inc. Bala Cynwyd, Pennsylvania	SDS-940	CAL, BASIC, QED, TAP, DDT, FORTRAN II, IV	TT-33, 35	32
Computer Sharing Services Denver, Colorado	GE-265	BASIC, FORTRAN II	TT-33, 35	see remarks
Computer Time-Sharing, Inc. Bloomington, Minnesota	CDC-3300	FORTRAN II, EDIT, DEBUG, BASIC	TT-33, 35	64
Com-Share, Inc. Chicago, Illinois	SDS 940	BASIC, CAL, QED, FORTRAN II, IV, DDT, TAP, SNOBOL	TT-33, 35, 37, PLT	32
Data Central, Inc. St. Louis, Missouri	SDS 940	BASIC, FORTRAN II, IV	TT-33, 35	32
Data Network Corp. New York, New York	SDS 940	BASIC, CAL, FORTRAN II, IV	TT-33, 35	32
DIAL-DATA, Inc. Newton, Massachusetts	SDS 940	CAL, DDT, QED, ALGOL, FORTRAN II, IV, BASIC, SNOBOL, ARPAS, LISP	TT-33, 35, 37, PLT, CRT	40
Direct Access Computer Corp. Southfield, Michigan	B-5500	ALGOL, BASIC, COBOL, FORTRAN IV	TT-33, 35	48
Fulton National Bank Atlanta, Georgia	GE-420	BASIC, FORTRAN IV	TT-33, 35	30
General Electric Co. Information Service Dept. Bethesda, Maryland	GE-265, 635	BASIC, ALGOL, FORTRAN II, IV	TT-33, 35, PLT, Friden 7100, 7102	40
Graphic Controls Buffalo, New York	GE-235	BASIC, ALGOL, EDIT, FORTRAN, PACER, TSAP, LAFFF, LISP	TT-33, 35, Friden 7100, 7102	40
IBM Information Marketing Dept. White Plains, New York	IBM 7044 360/40, 360/50	QUIKTRAN, 360 BASIC, 360 DATATEXT	IBM 1050, 2741, TT-33, 35	

HOURLY TERMINAL RATE	PROCESSOR TIME PER MINUTE	DISC STORAGE/ CUSTOMER	MINIMUM CHARGE PER MO.	REMARKS
None	$5.00-$10.00	0+	None	360/50 has been modified with special operation codes for efficient conversational interaction. CPU charges are dependent on amount of core used.
$10-$25	see remarks	10K+	None	Processor time is charged at $.015 for each 10,000 instructions executed.
$10-$15	$0-$25.00	50K+	None	TELCOMP available now — all other languages available in early 1969. No CPU charge for PDP-7, CPU charge for PDP-10 is $25 per minute.
$6.25-$12.75	$2.00	0+	$0-$250	A maximum of 30 users can be accommodated on a GE-420.
$6.50-$9.00	$3.00	0+	None	Special rates for high schools and colleges.
$7.00-$10.00	$12.00	75K+	None	System has capability of interfacing with high speed CDC 200 terminals.
$7.00-$10.00	$2.50	60K+	None	Terminal rates are increased by $3 per hour for the use of QED, BASIC, CAL, FORTRAN IV and DDT.
see remarks	see remarks	see remarks	see remarks	Rates are not presently available.
$10.00	$4.80	0+	None	Special rates available for large storage requirements and for heavy usage.
$10-$20	$2.50	60K+	$100.00	Com-Share Southern, Inc., an affiliate of Com-Share, Inc., has a different rate structure.
see remarks	see remarks	see remarks	see remarks	Rates are not presently available.
$9.00-$18.00	None	0+	$100.00	
$10-$12	$3.00	60K+	None	Special applications packages for Electronic Circuit Design and Analysis, Statistics, Linear Programming, etc.
see remarks	see remarks	see remarks	see remarks	Rates are not presently available.
$10.00	$3.00	0+	$350.00	I/O time is charged at the rate of $.03 per second.
$10.00	see remarks	0+	$100.00	ALGOL available with 265 only. FORTRAN IV available with 635 only. 64 users with 635. CPU rate for 265 is $24 per minute. 635 rate is $.40 per second.
$10-$13	$3.00	0+	$50.00	
see remarks	see remarks	0+	$100.00	Rates: Terminal/QUIKTRAN — $10/hr., DATATEXT — $2.15/hr., BASIC — $11/hr.; Processor/QUIKTRAN — $2/min., BASIC — $7/min., DATATEXT — $.008/7 I/O Transfers or 120 ms of processor time.

COMMERCIAL TIME-SHARING SYSTEMS

ORGANIZATION	COMPUTER	LANGUAGES	TERMINALS	NO. OF USERS
ITT Data Services Paramus, New Jersey	IBM 360/50, 360/65	FORTRAN IV, BASIC	TT-33,35 IBM 1050, 2741	50
Intinco Limited London, England	UNIVAC 418(2)	Stockbrokers Language	TT-33, 35	see remarks
John P. Maguire & Co., Inc. New York, New York	IBM 360/40	BTAM, DOS	IBM 1050, 2740	60
Keydata Corp. Watertown, Massachusetts	UNIVAC 491	KOP III, SPURT	TT-28	200
McDonnell Automation Co. St. Louis, Missouri	GE-420	BASIC, FORTRAN	TT-33, 35, Friden 7100	30
On-Line Systems, Inc. North Hills Pittsburgh, Pennsylvania	GE-255	BASIC, ALGOL, FORTRAN	TT-33, 35	20
Philco-Ford Corp. C. & E. Division Computer Services Network Willow Grove, Pennsylvania	B-3500, GE-265, Philco-212	BASIC, ALGOL, TUTOR, COBOL, FORTRAN II, IV	TT-33, 35, 37, Univac 1004, 1005, 1130	40
Pillsbury Management Systems Phoenix, Arizona	DATANET-30	TRAC	TT-33, 35, 37, IBM 2741	15
Rapidata New York, New York	GE-425 DATANET-30	BASIC, RITE, FORTRAN IV	TT-33, 35, Friden 7200, IBM 2741	40
REALTIME Systems, Inc. New York, New York	B-5500	FORTRAN IV, COBOL, ALGOL	TT-33, 35	24
Remote Computing Corp. Los Angeles, California	B-5500	COBOL, ALGOL, FORTRAN, BASIC	TT-33, 35	48
Time-Sharing Systems, Inc. Milwaukee, Wisconsin	B-5500	FORTRAN IV, ALGOL	TT-33, 35	32
TYMSHARE, Inc. Los Altos, California	SDS 940	CAL, BASIC, ARPAS, SUPER BASIC, QED, FORTRAN II, IV	TT-33, 35, 37, PLT, CRT, CR	42
U.S. Time Sharing, Inc. Washington, D.C.	IBM 360/50	360 ASSEMBLER, PL/1, FORTRAN IV, COBOL, RPG, ALGOL	TT-33, 35, IBM 1050, 2740, 2741, 2780, DURA 1021, 1041, CRT, Datel Thirty 21	67
Univac Information Services Div. Blue Bell, Pennsylvania	1108, 418, 9300	FORTRAN, COBOL SIMSCRIPT, GPSS	Univac 1004	see remarks
VIP Systems Corp. Washington, D.C.	IBM 1460	IBM ATS	IBM 2741, DATEL, DURA	40
White, Weld & Co. New York, New York	SDS 940	FFL, QED, DDT, FORTRAN II	TT-33, 35	24

HOURLY TERMINAL RATE	PROCESSOR TIME PER MINUTE	DISC STORAGE/ CUSTOMER	MINIMUM CHARGE PER MO.	REMARKS
$12.00	$7.00	0+	$150.00	Application packages for Consumer Credit Record Retrieval, Finance Accounting, and Mutual Fund Shareholder Accounting.
see remarks	see remarks	see remarks	see remarks	Methods of charging vary; the rate is approximately $5000 per year plus a usage charge of $.05 per inquiry.
see remarks	see remarks	see remarks	$1,500.00	All prices negotiated according to storage and processing requirements. System used for accounting and management services.
see remarks	see remarks	see remarks	see remarks	Charges based on message transmissions, processor time and storage. System used for accounting and management services.
$10.00	$3.00	0+	$100.00	
$12.50	None	0+	None	PDP-10 system under development.
$5.00-$15.00	$2.40-$5.00	0+	$100.00	Philco 212 system has no disc or drum storage.
$5.00	$.60-$1.20	0+	$100.00	System includes Test Editors, Management Information Systems and computer-assisted learning programs. Processor rates vary according to system used.
$9.00-$11.00	$3.00	0+	$100.00	I/O is charged at the rate of $.03 per second based on disc swap time.
$15.00	$6.65-$8.35	0+	$500.00	Several background jobs can be initiated by user to run concurrently.
$5.00	$6.00	0+	None	
$11.00	$7.20	see remarks	$75-$350	60K character of storage included in $350 per month minimum rate.
$13-$16	None	60K+	$80.00 or $390.00	Applications packages include COGO, ECAP, EASYPLOT, APT and CSMP.
$4.00-$6.00	$6.00-$9.00	0+	None	50,000 bytes of storage available at no additional cost for each $100 of usage per month.
see remarks	see remarks	see remarks	see remarks	Rates and user information not available at this time.
$5.00-$10.00	None	0+	$125-$800	Several rate plans available depending upon usage and terminal location. IBM 360/40 system is being planned.
see remarks	see remarks	see remarks	$1,500.00	Rate and storage information not available.

189

Table 3-3   Time sharing vendor data sheets. (Reproduced from Time-Sharing Industry Directory by permission of Time-Sharing Enterprises, Inc., King of Prussia, Pennsylvania.) (* Denotes vendors added since last update.)

page	vendor name
A-1.0	Academy Computing Corporation
A-2.0	Access Systems, Inc.
A-3.0	Allen-Babcock Computing, Inc.
A-4.0	American Fletcher National Bank and Trust Company (Call-A-Computer)
A-5.0	Applied Logic Corporation
A-6.0	Applied Time-Sharing, Inc.
A-7.0	AVCO Computer Services
A-8.0	Applied Computer Time Share, Inc.
A-9.0	American Computer & Communications Co.
A-10.0	Applied Digital Systems, Inc.
A-11.0*	APL—Manhattan
B-1.0	Basic Computing Arts, Inc. (Applied Logic Corporation)
B-2.0	Beverly Bank (Call-A-Computer)
B-3.0	Bolt, Beranek & Newman, Inc. (Telcomp)
B-4.0	Burlington Management Services, Co.
B-5.0	Braddock, Dunn & McDonald, Inc.
C-1.0	Call-A-Computer
C-2.0	Call-A-Computer of the Southeast, Inc. ☆☆ DELETE ☆☆
C-3.0	C-E-I-R
C-4.0	Central Computing, Inc.
C-5.0	Central Information Processing Corporation (Commercial Credit Corporation)
C-6.0	Chi Corporation
C-7.0	Collins Radio ☆☆ DELETE ☆☆
C-8.0	Community Computer Corporation
C-9.0	Computer Center Corporation
C-10.0	Computer Center of Southern New England (Call-A-Computer)
C-11.0	Computer Dynamics, Inc. (Applied Logic Corporation)
C-12.0	Computer Network Corporation (COMNET)
C-13.0	DELETED: Computer Programming Concepts, Inc.: March 1969 updates
C-14.0	Computer Response Corporation
C-15.0	Computer Science Corporation
C-16.0	Computer Sharing, Inc. (Scientific Resources Corporation)

page	vendor name
C-17.0	Computer Sharing Services
C-18.0	Computer Software Systems, Inc.
C-19.0	Computer Solutions, Inc. (Applied Logic Corporation)
C-20.0	Computer Technologies, Inc.
C-21.0*	Computility, Inc.
C-22.0	Computer Update, Inc.
C-23.0	Compu-Time, Inc.
C-24.0	Computrol Systems, Inc.
C-25.0	Com-Share, Inc.
C-26.0	Computer Complex, Inc. (formerly Com-Share Southern, Inc.)
C-27.0	Conley Corporation (Call-A-Computer)
C-28.0	Control Data Corporation
C-29.0	Computer Power, Inc.
C-30.0	Computer Time-Sharing Corporation
C-31.0	Computer Processing by Communication, Inc.
C-32.0*	COMSERV
C-33.0*	Call-A-Computer of California (Call-A-Computer)
C-34.0*	Cyphernetics Corporation
C-35.0*	Call-A-Computer of Cincinnati (Call-A-Computer)
C-36.0*	Computer Task Group, Inc. (Applied Logic)
D-1.0	Data Central, Inc.
D-2.0	Data Research Corporation (Ozark-Mahoning Co.)
D-3.0	Datalogics, Inc. (Globe Life Corporation)
D-4.0	Datametrics Corporation ☆☆ DELETE ☆☆
D-5.0	Data Network Corporation
D-6.0	Davis Computer Systems, Inc. (Applied Logic)
D-7.0	Delmarva Associates (Call-A-Computer)
D-8.0	Dial-Data, Inc.
D-9.0	Digitek Time-Share, Inc.
D-10.0	Direct Access Computing Corporation
D-11.0	Dyna Com, Inc. ☆☆ DELETE ☆☆
D-12.0	Directed Research, Inc. (Applied Logic)
D-13.0*	DIALOG Computing, Inc.
E-1.0	EDP Central, Inc.
E-2.0	E. D. P. Com-Share, Inc. (Com-Share Southern, Inc.)
E-3.0	E. L. I. Computer Time-Sharing
F-1.0	Financial Computer Service, Inc.

page	vendor name

F-2.0   Fulton National Bank

G-1.0   General Computer Services, Inc.   ☆☆   DELETE   ☆☆
G-2.0   General Electric Company
G-3.0   Graphic Controls Corporation
G-4.0   Greyhound Time-Sharing
G-5.0*   Genessee Computer Center, Inc.

H-1.0   Honeywell, Inc.
H-2.0*   Hobbs Associates

I-1.0   I-C Computer Corporation
I-2.0   Ikon Data Systems
I-3.0   Information Management Corporation (Applied Logic)
I-4.0   Information Network Corporation
I-5.0   Information Systems Corporation (Applied Logic)
I-6.0   Insta-Com of Florida   ☆☆   DELETE   ☆☆
I-7.0   Integon Computer Corporation
I-8.0   Interactive Computing Corporation
I-9.0   Interactive Data Corporation
I-10.0   Interactive Sciences Corporation
I-11.0   Interface Computer, Inc.
I-12.0   International Telecomputer Network Corporation
I-13.0   ITT Data Services
I-14.0   Information and Computing Centers Corporation
I-15.0   Interaccess Corporation
I-16.0   International Time-Sharing Corporation
         (formerly Computer Time-Sharing, Inc.)
I-17.0   Intranet Industries, Inc. (formerly Information Industries, Inc.)
I-18.0*   Intelecom, Inc.

K-1.0   John A. Keane and Associates (Applied Logic Corporation)
K-2.0   Keydata Corporation (formerly Keydata & Adams Associates, Inc.)
K-3.0   KPA Time-Sharing, Inc. (Applied Logic Corporation)
K-4.0*   Kentucky Data Systems
         (Call-A-Computer)

L-1.0   Leasco Systems and Research Corporation
L-2.0   Lovell Enterprises   ☆☆   DELETE   ☆☆

M-1.0   John P. Maguire & Company, Inc.
M-2.0   Marketing Operations, Inc.
         (Call-A-Computer)
M-3.0   Management Information Services, Inc.
M-4.0   Marquardt Corporation (CCI Marquardt Corporation)

page	vendor name
M-5.0	The Matrix Corporation
M-6.0	McDonnell Automation Company
M-7.0	Metridata Computing, Inc. (formerly Datametrics, Inc.)
M-8.0	Multi Access Computing Inc.
N-1.0	National Cash Register
N-2.0	New England Merchants National Bank (Call-A-Computer)
N-3.0	Northwest Management Services, Inc.
O-1.0	On-Line Systems, Inc.
P-1.0	Philco-Ford Corporation
P-2.0	Piedmont Call-A-Computer, Inc. (Call-A-Computer)
P-3.0	Pittsburgh National Bank
P-4.0	PRC Computer Center, Inc. (Planning Research Corporation)
P-5.0	Princeton Time-Sharing Services, Inc.
P-6.0	Programs and Analysis, Inc.
P-7.0*	Pryor Computer Time-Sharing Corporation
R-1.0	Rapidata
R-2.0	Realtime Systems, Inc.
R-3.0	Remote Computing Corporation
R-4.0*	L. R. Reeves Company
S-1.0	Scientific Data Systems, Inc.
S-2.0	Service Bureau Corporation
S-3.0	Shared Computer Systems Corporation
S-4.0	Statistical Tabulating Corporation
S-5.0	Systems Science Corporation
S-6.0	Sci-Tek Computer Centers, Inc.
S-7.0	Strategic Time-Sharing, Inc.
S-8.0	System Development Corporation
S-9.0*	Systems Analysis Company (Call-A-Computer)
T-1.0	Technical Advisors, Inc.
T-2.0	Tel-A-Data, Inc.
T-3.0	Time Share Corporation
T-4.0	Time-Sharing Systems, Inc.
T-5.0	Tracor Computing Corporation
T-6.0	Tymshare, Inc.
T-7.0	Telecomputations, Inc.
T-8.0*	Technology for Information Management, Inc.
T-9.0*	Transdata Corporation

bibliography

Adams, Charles W., "The Meanings of Time-Sharing." A pamphlet distributed by Charles W. Adams, Chairman, at the Panel Discussion on The Meanings of Time-Sharing, Spring Joint Computer Conference, Boston, Mass., April 27, 1966.

————, "On-line Time-Sharing: Its Potential for Management." Address given at the Management Conference, Business Equipment Manufacturers Association, Chicago, October 24, 1967.

Anderson, B.R., *et al., Future of the Computer Utility*. New York: American Management Association, 1967.

Duggan, Michael A., "Computer Utilities—Social and Policy Implications: A Reference Bibliography," *Computing Reviews* (Association for Computing Machinery), VII, No. 10 (October, 1968).

"Information Becomes a Hot Item," *Business Week*, (May 14, 1966).

"The Information Explosion: The Computer in Society," *The General Electric Forum*, X, No. 4 (Winter, 1967–68).

Main, Jeremy, "Computer Time-Sharing—Everyman at the Console," *Fortune*, LXXVI (August, 1967).

Martin, J., *Telecommunications and the Computer*. Englewood Cliffs, New Jersey: Prentice-Hall, Inc., 1969.

Mathison, Stuart L. and Philip M. Walker, *Computers and Telecommunications: Issues in Public Policy*. Englewood Cliffs, N.J.: Prentice-Hall, Inc., 1969.

Parkhill, D.F., *Challenge of the Computer Utility*. Reading, Mass.: Addison-Wesley Publishing Co., 1966.

Spiegel, Joe, "The Electronic Executive." In the Proceedings of the Spring Joint Computer Conference, Boston, Mass., April 27, 1966.

Sprague, Richard E., *Electronic Business Systems*. New York: The Ronald Press Company, 1962.

Time-Sharing Industry Directory. King of Prussia, Pa.: Time-Sharing Enterprises, Inc., 1968

Time-Sharing System Scorecard. Newton, Mass.: Computer Research Corp., 1968

index

197